# TEEN RIGHTS AND FREEDOMS

# Free Speech and Expression

TEEN RIGHTS AND FREEDOMS

# Free Speech and Expression

Noël Merino
*Book Editor*

**GREENHAVEN PRESS**
*A part of Gale, Cengage Learning*

GALE
CENGAGE Learning·

Detroit • New York • San Francisco • New Haven, Conn • Waterville, Maine • London

Elizabeth Des Chenes, *Managing Editor*

© 2012 Greenhaven Press, a part of Gale, Cengage Learning

Gale and Greenhaven Press are registered trademarks used herein under license.

For more information, contact:
Greenhaven Press
27500 Drake Rd.
Farmington Hills, MI 48331-3535
Or you can visit our Internet site at gale.cengage.com.

For product information and technology assistance, contact us at:

Gale Customer Support, 1-800-877-4253.
For permission to use material from this text or product, submit all requests online at www.cengage.com/permissions.

Further permissions questions can be emailed to permissionrequest@cengage.com.

Articles in Greenhaven Press anthologies are often edited for length to meet page requirements. In addition, original titles of these works are changed to clearly present the main thesis and to explicitly indicate the author's opinion. Every effort is made to ensure the Greenhaven Press accurately reflects the original intent of the authors. Every effort has been made to trace the owners of copyrighted material.

Cover Image © Molly Riley/Reuters

**LIBRARY OF CONGRESS CATALOGING-IN-PUBLICATION DATA**

Free speech and expression / Noël Merino, book editor.
   p. cm. -- (Teen rights and freedoms)
  Includes bibliographical references and index.
  ISBN 978-0-7377-5826-9 (hardcover : alk. paper)
1. Freedom of speech--United States--Popular works. 2. College students--Legal status, laws, etc.--United States--Popular works. 3. College students--Civil rights--United States--Popular works. 4. High school students--Legal status, laws, etc.--United States--Popular works. 5. High school students--Civil rights--United States--Popular works. I. Merino, Noël.
  KF4772.F736 2008
  342.7308'53--dc22
                                     2011015671

Printed in the United States of America
1 2 3 4 5 6 7 15 14 13 12 11

# Contents

*American Civil Liberties Union*

The American Civil Liberties Union recounts many of the key struggles in the United States' advancement of freedom of expression and emphasizes its importance.

*Emily Buss*

A law professor illustrates the way children's right to freedom of expression differs from that of adults by considering several Supreme Court cases on the issue.

*Robert H. Jackson*

The US Supreme Court determines that, because of their right to free expression, students are not allowed to be disciplined for failing to salute the flag and recite the pledge.

*Abe Fortas*

The US Supreme Court rules that students must be allowed to express their opinions as long as doing so does not cause substantial disorder or interfere with school activities.

*Warren E. Burger*

The US Supreme Court decides that the right to free speech does not prevent schools from limiting student speech that is disruptive because of its lewdness.

*Byron White*

The US Supreme Court rules that schools have a right to control student speech when it is associated with an activity that is part of the school curriculum.

*James Tidwell*

A journalism professor praises a Sixth Circuit Court of Appeals decision that college students cannot have their freedom of expression limited in the same manner as high school students.

*John Roberts*

The US Supreme Court rules that student expression that appears to advocate illegal drug use is not protected under the First Amendment.

*Perry A. Zirkel*

A professor of education and law interviews three former plaintiffs from important First Amendment cases addressing student speech.

*Stephen Roy Reinhardt*

A circuit court determines that it does not violate a student's First Amendment right to limit expression that interferes with the rights of other students.

*Greg Beato*

A writer contends that student speech on T-shirts at high school is an important exercise of free expression under the First Amendment and ought to be embraced.

*Theresa Chmara*

A lawyer contends that the First Amendment right to free expression that is extended to students includes the

right of access to information, which must be protected by
school libraries.

# Foreword

*"In the truest sense freedom cannot be
bestowed, it must be achieved."*
Franklin D. Roosevelt,
September 16, 1936

The notion of children and teens having rights is a relatively recent development. Early in American history, the head of the household—nearly always the father—exercised complete control over the children in the family. Children were legally considered to be the property of their parents. Over time, this view changed, as society began to acknowledge that children have rights independent of their parents, and that the law should protect young people from exploitation. By the early twentieth century, more and more social reformers focused on the welfare of children, and over the ensuing decades advocates worked to protect them from harm in the workplace, to secure public education for all, and to guarantee fair treatment for youths in the criminal justice system. Throughout the twentieth century, rights for children and teens—and restrictions on those rights—were established by Congress and reinforced by the courts. Today's courts are still defining and clarifying the rights and freedoms of young people, sometimes expanding those rights and sometimes limiting them. Some teen rights are outside the scope of public law and remain in the realm of the family, while still others are determined by school policies.

Each volume in the Teen Rights and Freedoms series focuses on a different right or freedom and offers an anthology of key essays and articles on that right or freedom and the responsibilities that come with it. Material within each volume is drawn from a diverse selection of primary and secondary sources— journals, magazines, newspapers, nonfiction books, organization newsletters, position papers, speeches, and government documents, with a particular emphasis on Supreme Court and lower court decisions. Volumes also include first-person narratives from young people and others involved in teen rights issues, such as parents and educators. The material is selected and arranged to highlight all the major social and legal controversies relating to the right or freedom under discussion. Each selection is preceded by an introduction that provides context and background. In many cases, the essays point to the difference between adult and teen rights, and why this difference exists.

Many of the volumes cover rights guaranteed under the Bill of Rights and how these rights are interpreted and protected in regard to children and teens, including freedom of speech, freedom of the press, due process, and religious rights. The scope of the series also encompasses rights or freedoms, whether real or perceived, relating to the school environment, such as electronic devices, dress, Internet policies, and privacy. Some volumes focus on the home environment, including topics such as parental control and sexuality.

Numerous features are included in each volume of Teen Rights and Freedoms:

- An annotated **table of contents** provides a brief summary of each essay in the volume and highlights court decisions and personal narratives.

- An **introduction** specific to the volume topic gives context for the right or freedom and its impact on daily life.

- A brief **chronology** offers important dates associated with the right or freedom, including landmark court cases.

- **Primary sources**—including personal narratives and court decisions—are among the varied selections in the anthology.

- **Illustrations**—including photographs, charts, graphs, tables, statistics, and maps—are closely tied to the text and chosen to help readers understand key points or concepts.

- An annotated list of **organizations to contact** presents sources of additional information on the topic.
- A **for further reading** section offers a bibliography of books, periodical articles, and Internet sources for further research.
- A comprehensive subject **index** provides access to key people, places, events, and subjects cited in the text.

Each volume of Teen Rights and Freedoms delves deeply into the issues most relevant to the lives of teens: their own rights, freedoms, and responsibilities. With the help of this series, students and other readers can explore from many angles the evolution and current expression of rights both historic and contemporary.

# Introduction

The constitutional rights of teens have expanded dramatically over the past century, notably with respect to the right to free speech and expression secured by the First Amendment to the US Constitution. The Free Speech Clause of the First Amendment guarantees, "Congress shall make no law . . . abridging the freedom of speech." The right to free speech is not absolute—there are restrictions. Additionally, the free speech rights of adults are broader than those of minors. Exactly what kind of expression the First Amendment protects and does not protect is an issue that has frequently made its way to court, and the highest court in the land—the US Supreme Court—has made several key decisions over the years that have determined how the Free Speech Clause of the First Amendment is to be interpreted, for adults and for minors.

The right to freedom of speech guaranteed by the First Amendment has never been absolute. In the early twentieth century, the Court heard a series of cases involving criticism of the government during World War I and determined that the government may place criminal sanctions on speech or expression that would "create a clear and present danger"[1] of unlawful or harmful conduct. In 1942, a unanimous Court defined several categories of speech that are not protected by the First Amendment:

> There are certain well-defined and narrowly limited classes of speech, the prevention and punishment of which have never been thought to raise any Constitutional problem. These include the lewd and obscene, the profane, the libelous, and the insulting or "fighting" words—those which, by their very utterance, inflict injury or tend to incite an immediate breach of the peace. It has been well observed that such utterances are no essential part of any exposition of ideas, and are of such slight social value as a step to truth that any benefit that may

be derived from them is clearly outweighed by the social interest in order and morality.[2]

Three broad categories stand out for unprotected speech: speech that is obscene, speech that publicly defames another person, and speech that incites lawlessness. The restriction on such speech has generally been progressively loosened over the last few decades.

Prior to the mid-twentieth century, the Court did not recognize the rights of minors. It treated children somewhat like the property of their parents. In the second half of the twentieth century, the Court began to speak about the rights of children under the Fourteenth Amendment to equal protection of the laws. Nonetheless, competing rights and interests limit the rights of minors. To this day, the rights of minors are often limited by the rights of parents to control the upbringing of their child and by the state's interest in protecting minors.

The free speech rights of minors are at issue most frequently within the school setting. In *West Virginia State Board of Education v. Barnette* (1943), the Court held that the First Amendment protected students from being forced to salute the American flag and recite the pledge of allegiance, thus protecting students' rights to abstain from certain speech. In protecting students' rights to actively engage in speech, the seminal case is *Tinker v. Des Moines Independent Community School District* (1969). *Tinker* involved three teenagers who wore black armbands to school in protest of the Vietnam War. Their schools had adopted a policy banning the wearing of armbands, in an attempt to avoid any conflict that might result from student protest. The Court in *Tinker* held that schools may not limit student speech simply due to a "wish to avoid the controversy which might result from the expression." The *Tinker* Court held that although school officials have the authority to limit conduct that would "materially and substantially interfere with the requirements of appropriate discipline in the operation of the school," they must show more than "a mere desire to avoid the discomfort and unpleasantness that always accompany an unpopular viewpoint."[3]

In cases since *Tinker*, the Court has expounded upon what kinds of issues constitute a material and substantial disruption, thus allowing school officials to limit the expression of students without violating the First Amendment. In the 1986 case of *Bethel School District v. Fraser*, the Court held that school officials may prohibit student speech that contains sexual innuendo. In the 1988 case of *Hazelwood School District v. Kuhlmeier*, the Court held that schools may regulate student speech in the school newspaper when done for legitimate educational reasons. And, most recently, the Court held in *Morse v. Frederick* (2007) that schools may prohibit both at school and at school events student expression that appears to advocate illegal drug use.

The free speech rights of teenagers continue to ignite controversy, with cases regularly going to court to determine how much freedom of expression young people are guaranteed and in what ways their First Amendment rights may be constitutionally limited. In recent years, with the advent of online social networking and other student speech on the Internet, schools are struggling to determine when and whether they may limit student speech that is not made at school but that impacts life at school. Other ongoing issues include the rights of students to express themselves through clothing, particularly when such expression is offensive to other students. The key student speech court cases and these other evolving issues are explored and debated in *Teen Rights and Freedoms: Free Speech and Expression*.

## Notes

1. *Schenck v. United States*, 249 US 47 (1919).
2. *Chaplinsky v. State of New Hampshire*, 315 US 568 (1942).
3. *Tinker v. Des Moines Independent Community School District*, 393 US 503 (1969).

# Chronology

**1791**      The United States adopts the Bill of Rights, whose First Amendment reads: "Congress shall make no law respecting an establishment of religion, or prohibiting the free exercise thereof; or abridging the freedom of speech, or of the press; or the right of the people peaceably to assemble, and to petition the Government for a redress of grievances."

**1940**      In *Minersville School District v. Gobitis* the Supreme Court rules that the rights of Jehovah's Witness students were not violated when they were required to salute the flag in public schools.

**1943**      In *West Virginia State Board of Education v. Barnette* the Supreme Court reverses the *Minersville School District v. Gobitis* decision and rules that a compulsory salute of the American flag by schoolchildren violates the First Amendment's Free Speech Clause.

**1968**      In *Ginsberg v. New York* the Supreme Court upholds a state law prohibiting the sale to minors of magazines containing nudity, where the sale of such magazines was permitted for adults.

**1968**      In *United States v. O'Brien* the Supreme Court rules that burning one's draft card as a statement of protest against the Vietnam War is not protected by the First Amendment.

**1969**   In *Tinker v. Des Moines Indpendent School District* the Supreme Court holds that the First Amendment protects public school students' rights to express political and social views.

**1973**   In *Miller v. California* the Supreme Court clarifies what counts as obscenity, which is not protected by the First Amendment, by defining it as something that appeals to prurient interests; describes sexual conduct in an offensive way; and has no literary, artistic, political, or scientific value.

**1982**   In *Board of Education v. Pico* the Supreme Court rules that students' First Amendment rights limit the school's authority to remove books from the school library.

**1986**   In *Bethel School District v. Fraser* the Supreme Court upholds the power of school officials to discipline a student for making a sexually aggressive (but not obscene) speech.

**1988**   In *Hazelwood School District v. Kuhlmeier* the Supreme Court rules that schools have a right to control student speech when it is associated with an activity that is part of the school curriculum.

**1989**　　In *Texas v. Johnson* the Supreme Court rules that citizens have the right to make a political statement by burning a privately owned US flag.

**1997**　　In *Reno v. American Civil Liberties Union* the Supreme Court strikes down the Communications Decency Act, which Congress had passed in an attempt to control Internet content.

**2003**　　In *United States v. American Library Association* the Supreme Court upholds the Children's Internet Protection Act, ruling that public libraries' use of Internet filtering software does not violate the First Amendment rights of library patrons.

**2006**　　In *Harper v. Poway Unified School District* the US Court of Appeals for the Ninth Circuit determines that it does not violate a student's First Amendment rights to limit antihomosexual expression when it interferes with the rights of other students.

**2007**　　In *Morse v. Frederick* the Supreme Court rules that student expression that appears to advocate illegal drugs is not protected under the First Amendment.

> "The nation's commitment to freedom of expression has been tested over and over again."

# Freedom of Expression Is a Fundamental Constitutional Right

## American Civil Liberties Union (ACLU)

*In the following viewpoint the American Civil Liberties Union (ACLU) argues that the freedom of expression guaranteed by the First Amendment of the US Constitution is one of the most fundamental constitutional freedoms. The ACLU recounts several struggles waged to protect this freedom, and the group cites several key US Supreme Court cases that helped to define and expand this freedom over the last century. It notes that freedom of expression applies to both pure and symbolic speech, as well as to unpopular hate speech. In addition, the ACLU identifies several types of speech that are not protected by the First Amendment. The ACLU is a national organization dedicated to defending and expanding all civil liberties and civil rights in America.*

Freedom of speech, of the press, of association, of assembly and petition—this set of guarantees, protected by the First Amendment, comprises what we refer to as freedom of expression. The Supreme Court has written that this freedom is "the matrix, the indispensable condition of nearly every other form of freedom." Without it, other fundamental rights, like the right to vote, would wither and die.

## First Amendment Struggles

But in spite of its "preferred position" in our constitutional hierarchy, the nation's commitment to freedom of expression has been tested over and over again. Especially during times of national stress, like war abroad or social upheaval at home, people exercising their First Amendment rights have been censored, fined, even jailed. Those with unpopular political ideas have always borne the brunt of government repression. It was during WWI—hardly ancient history—that a person could be jailed just for giving out anti-war leaflets. Out of those early cases, modern First Amendment law evolved. Many struggles and many cases later, ours is the most speech-protective country in the world.

The path to freedom was long and arduous. It took nearly 200 years to establish firm constitutional limits on the government's power to punish "seditious" and "subversive" speech. Many people suffered along the way, such as labor leader Eugene V. Debs, who was sentenced to 10 years in prison under the Espionage Act just for telling a rally of peaceful workers to realize they were "fit for something better than slavery and cannon fodder." Or Sidney Street, jailed in 1969 for burning an American flag on a Harlem street corner to protest the shooting of civil rights figure James Meredith.

Free speech rights still need constant, vigilant protection. New questions arise and old ones return. Should flag burning be a crime? What about government or private censorship of works of art that touch on sensitive issues like religion or sexuality? Should the Internet be subject to any form of government control? What about punishing college students who espouse racist or sexist opinions? In answering these questions, the history and the core values of the First Amendment should be our guide.

## The Supreme Court and the First Amendment

During our nation's early era, the courts were almost universally hostile to political minorities' First Amendment rights; free speech issues did not even reach the Supreme Court until 1919 when, in *Schenck v. U.S.*, the Court unanimously upheld the conviction of a Socialist Party member for mailing anti-war leaflets to draft-age men. A turning point occurred a few months later in *Abrams v. U.S.* Although the defendant's conviction under the Espionage Act for distributing anti-war leaflets was upheld, two dissenting opinions formed the cornerstone of our modern First Amendment law. Justices Oliver Wendell Holmes and Louis D. Brandeis argued speech could *only* be punished *if* it presented "a clear and present danger" of imminent harm. Mere political advocacy, they said, was protected by the First Amendment. Eventually, these justices were able to convince a majority of the Court to adopt the "clear and present danger test."

From then on, the right to freedom of expression grew more secure—until the 1950s and McCarthyism. The Supreme Court fell prey to the witch-hunt mentality of that period, seriously weakening the "clear and present danger" test by holding that speakers could be punished if they advocated overthrowing the government—even if the danger of such an occurrence were both slight and remote. As a result, many political activists were prosecuted and jailed simply for advocating communist revolution. Loyalty oath requirements for government employees were upheld; thousands of Americans lost their jobs on the basis of flimsy evidence supplied by secret witnesses.

Finally, in 1969, in *Brandenberg v. Ohio*, the Supreme Court struck down the conviction of a Ku Klux Klan member and established a new standard: Speech can be suppressed only if it is intended, *and likely to produce*, "imminent lawless action." Otherwise, even speech that advocates violence is protected. The Brandenberg standard prevails today.

## Pure Speech and Symbolic Speech

First Amendment protection is not limited to "pure speech"— books, newspapers, leaflets and rallies. It also "protects symbolic speech"—nonverbal expression whose purpose is to communicate ideas. In its 1969 decision in *Tinker v. Des Moines*, the Court recognized the right of public school students to wear black armbands in protest of the Vietnam War. In 1989 (*Texas v. Johnson*) and again in 1990 (*U.S. v. Eichman*), the Court struck down government bans on "flag desecration." Other examples of protected symbolic speech include works of art, T-shirt slogans, political buttons, music lyrics and theatrical performances.

Government can limit some protected speech by imposing "time, place and manner" restrictions. This is most commonly

*Black arm bands such as those at issue in the* Tinker *case are commonly used as signs of protest.* © Jay Directo/AFP /Getty Images.

done by requiring permits for meetings, rallies and demonstrations. But a permit cannot be unreasonably withheld, nor can it be denied based on content of the speech. That would be what is called viewpoint discrimination—and *that* is unconstitutional.

When a protest crosses the line from speech to action, the government can intervene more aggressively. Political protesters have the right to picket, to distribute literature, to chant and to engage passersby in debate. But they do not have the right to block building entrances or to physically harass people.

## The Free Speech Clause

The First Amendment to the U.S. Constitution provides that "Congress shall make no law . . . abridging the freedom of speech." The rights protected under the First Amendment are among the freedoms most cherished by Americans. Democratic societies by definition are participatory and deliberative. They are designed to work best when their representative assemblies conduct informed deliberation after voters voice their opinions about particular issues or controversies. But neither elected representatives nor their constituents can fully discharge their democratic responsibilities if they are prevented from freely exchanging their thoughts, theories, suspicions, beliefs and ideas, or are hindered from gaining access to relevant facts, data or other kinds of useful information upon which to form their opinions.

The theory underlying the Free Speech Clause of the First Amendment is that truthful and accurate information can only be revealed through robust and uninhibited discourse, and that the best way to combat false, deceptive, misleading, inaccurate or hateful speech is with countervailing speech that ultimately carries the day with a majority of the populace and its elected representatives.

*"Free Speech/Free Expression,"* Gale Encyclopedia of Law, *Ed. Jeffrey Wilson. 2nd ed., vol. 1, Detroit: Gale, 2006.*

# Free Speech for Hatemongers?

The ACLU [American Civil Liberties Union] has often been at the center of controversy for defending the free speech rights of groups that spew hate, such as the Ku Klux Klan and the Nazis. But if only popular ideas were protected, we wouldn't need a First Amendment. History teaches that the first target of government repression is never the last. If we do not come to the defense of the free speech rights of the most unpopular among us, even if their views are antithetical to the very freedom the First Amendment stands for, then no one's liberty will be secure. In that sense, all First Amendment rights are "indivisible."

Censoring so-called hate speech also runs counter to the long-term interests of the most frequent victims of hate: racial, ethnic, religious and sexual minorities. We should not give the government the power to decide which opinions are hateful, for history has taught us that government is more apt to use this power to prosecute minorities than to protect them. As one federal judge has put it, tolerating hateful speech is "the best protection we have against any Nazi-type regime in this country."

At the same time, freedom of speech does not prevent punishing conduct that intimidates, harasses or threatens another person, even if words are used. Threatening phone calls, for example, are not constitutionally protected.

## Speech and National Security

The Supreme Court has recognized the government's interest in keeping some information secret, such as wartime troop deployments. But the Court has never actually upheld an injunction against speech on national security grounds. Two lessons can be learned from this historical fact. First, the amount of speech that can be curtailed in the interest of national security is very limited. And second, the government has historically overused the concept of "national security" to shield itself from criticism, and to discourage public discussion of controversial policies or decisions.

In 1971, the publication of the "Pentagon Papers" by the *New York Times* brought the conflicting claims of free speech and national security to a head. The Pentagon Papers, a voluminous secret history and analysis of the country's involvement in Vietnam, was leaked to the press. When the *Times* ignored the government's demand that it cease publication, the stage was set for a Supreme Court decision. In the landmark *U.S. v. New York Times* case, the Court ruled that the government could not, through "prior restraint," block publication of any material unless it could prove that [the material] would "surely" result in "direct, immediate, and irreparable" harm to the nation. This the government failed to prove, and the public was given access to vital information about an issue of enormous importance.

The public's First Amendment "right to know" is essential to its ability to fully participate in democratic decision-making. As the Pentagon Papers case demonstrates, the government's claims of "national security" must always be closely scrutinized to make sure they are valid.

## Unprotected Expression

The Supreme Court has recognized several limited exceptions to First Amendment protection.

In *Chaplinsky v. New Hampshire* (1942), the Court held that so-called "fighting words . . . which by their very utterance inflict injury or tend to incite an immediate breach of the peace," are not protected. This decision was based on the fact that fighting words are of "slight social value as a step to truth."

In *New York Times Co. v. Sullivan* (1964), the Court held that defamatory falsehoods about public officials can be punished— *only* if the offended official can prove the falsehoods were published with "actual malice," i.e.: "knowledge that the statement was false or with reckless disregard of whether it was false or not." Other kinds of "libelous statements" are also punishable.

Legally "obscene" material has historically been excluded from First Amendment protection. Unfortunately, the relatively narrow obscenity exception, described below, has been abused by government authorities and private pressure groups. Sexual expression in art and entertainment is, and has historically been, the most frequent target of censorship crusades, from James Joyce's classic *Ulysses* to the photographs of Robert Mapplethorpe.

In the 1973 *Miller v. California* decision, the Court established three conditions that must be present if a work is to be deemed "legally obscene." It must (1) appeal to the average person's prurient (shameful, morbid) interest in sex; (2) depict sexual conduct in a "patently offensive way" as defined by community standards; and (3) taken as a whole, lack serious literary, artistic, political or scientific value. Attempts to apply the "Miller test" have demonstrated the impossibility of formulating a precise definition of obscenity. Justice Potter Stewart once delivered a famous one-liner on the subject: "I know it when I see it." But the fact is, the obscenity exception to the First Amendment is highly subjective and practically invites government abuse.

"*The Supreme Court has made clear that the First Amendment of the U.S. Constitution, like other constitutional rights, applies to children.*"

# The First Amendment Rights of Children Differ from Those of Adults

**Emily Buss**

*In the following viewpoint Emily Buss contends that although children have First Amendment rights, these rights are not exactly the same as adults' First Amendment rights. She notes that most of the US Supreme Court's rulings on the First Amendment rights of minors have to do with their rights of expression in school. She recounts several key cases that expanded the speech rights of students and several that have restricted student rights to free expression. She also explains how the Supreme Court has identified children's right under the First Amendment to have access to information. Emily Buss is the Mark and Barbara Fried Professor of Law at the University of Chicago Law School.*

The Supreme Court has made clear that the First Amendment of the U.S. Constitution, like other constitutional rights, applies to children. The scope and nature of those rights, however, differs considerably from the First Amendment rights of adults. This difference is, in part, attributed to children's lesser maturity, which may compromise their ability to understand the potential negative effects of their speech on others and also make them more vulnerable to those effects themselves. At least as important is the different context in which children's First Amendment claims arise. Most of the Supreme Court's rulings on children's First Amendment rights address children's rights of expression in school, where the Court has recognized a strong state interest in controlling curriculum and student behavior.

## Cases Expanding Student Speech

The earliest student speech case, *West Virginia State Board of Education v. Barnette* (1943), held that students could not be compelled to salute the flag in violation of their personal beliefs. Writing for the majority, Justice Robert Jackson noted the connection between affording children expressive freedom in school and nurturing their development into effective participants in a democratic system of government: "That [schools] are educating the young for citizenship is reason for scrupulous protection of constitutional freedoms of the individual, if we are not to strangle the free mind at its source and teach youth to discount important principles of our government as mere platitudes."

A quarter century later, in *Tinker v. Des Moines School District* (1969), the Court held that the suspension of several students for wearing black armbands to school in protest of the United States' military involvement in Vietnam violated their First Amendment rights. In a decision by Justice Abe Fortas, the Court famously declared that "it can hardly be argued that either students or teachers shed their constitutional rights to freedom of speech or expression at the schoolhouse gate." *Tinker* directed that student speech was to be protected unless it "materially disrupts class work or involves substantial disorder or invasion of the rights of others."

*Tinker* was understood, at the time, to provide broad protection to students' right to free expression in school, and it inspired considerable litigation and changes in schools' policy. But in the three major cases that subsequently reached the Supreme Court, the students' speech claims were rejected.

## Cases Restricting Student Speech

In *Bethel School District No. 403 v. Fraser* (1986), a high school student was suspended for using "offensively lewd and indecent" language and gestures during a speech before an assembly of the entire student body. Despite the fact that an equivalent speech made by adults in a public setting would be protected, the Supreme Court upheld the school's action. In doing so, it emphasized that the school had an important role to play in teaching students "the habits and manners of civility," required to maintain a democratic system of government. In justifying its decision, it noted both that the speech in question had no political message and that it might have been "seriously damaging" to students, particularly younger female students, who could be confused or insulted by its message.

In *Hazelwood School District v. Kuhlmeier* (1988), a high school principal banned publication of two pages of a student newspaper because he determined that two articles on those pages inadequately protected the interests of some of the articles' subjects. The Supreme Court upheld the principal's actions, despite the paper's declared policy announcing that the paper "accepts all rights implied by the First Amendment . . . [and understands that only speech that meets the *Tinker* standard] can be prohibited." Central to the Court's holding was the fact that the paper was funded by the school and produced as part of a journalism class, where a teacher assigned articles to students, reviewed student work, and awarded grades and credit. As a sponsor of the speech, which had a curricular purpose, the school

*Members of the group "Sensible Drug Policy" demonstrated outside the US Supreme Court while the Court heard arguments in* Morse v. Frederick. © Mark Wilson/Getty Images.

was given wide latitude to control its content, subject only to the "reasonableness" constraint associated with speech limitations in nonpublic forums.

In *Morse v. Frederick* (2007), a principal suspended a high school student for unfurling a banner with the phrase "BONG HiTS 4 JESUS" outside the school in front of other students who had been dismissed from classes to join spectators watching the Olympic torch pass by their school. Again the Court upheld the suspension. In his decision Chief Justice John Roberts noted that the banner could readily be interpreted to promote illegal drug use and stressed the state's strong interest in deterring drug use by its students. The Court suggested that, had the banner conveyed some message related to the ongoing political debate about the legalization of marijuana, it might well have been protected. In announcing its decision, the *Morse* Court emphasized that *Tinker's* highly protective standard was limited to students' independent speech, particularly political speech, and noted that the Court had allowed other interests to come into play in *Fraser*

## The Rights of Students

Public school students do not lose their constitutional rights when they walk through the schoolhouse doors. The U.S. Supreme Court has recognized that "students in school as well as out of school are 'persons' under our Constitution." This means that they possess First Amendment rights to express themselves in a variety of ways. They can write articles for the school newspaper, join clubs, distribute literature and petition school officials.

But public school students do not possess unlimited First Amendment rights. Two legal principles limit their rights. First, as the Supreme Court has said, minors do not possess the same level of constitutional rights as adults. Second, the government generally has greater power to dictate policy when it acts in certain capacities, such as educator, employer or jailer.

*David L. Hudson Jr., "Student Expression: Overview," First Amendment Center, no date.*

(where the speech was frivolous and offensive) and *Hazelwood* (where student views could be mistaken for the views of the school).

## Children's Right of Access to Information

The Supreme Court has also addressed children's right to access information, but this area of law is less well developed. In *Ginsberg v. New York* (1968), the Court upheld a state law that prohibited the sale to minors of magazines that could not have been censored for adults. Decided just one year before *Tinker,* *Ginsberg* noted, generally, that "the power of the state to control the conduct of children reaches beyond the scope of its authority over adults," quoting *Prince v. Massachusetts* (1944) and, more specifically, that the state had an interest in supporting parents in the upbringing of their children and an independent interest in protecting children from harm. In *Board of Education, Island Trees Union Free School District No. 26 v. Pico* (1982), a plurality of the Court ruled that students' First Amendment rights limit the school's authority to remove books from the school library, particularly if that removal is motivated by a disapproval of the views expressed in the books. While children's right to access information and images on the Internet have also been asserted alongside adult claims in cases challenging Internet regulations, the Supreme Court has focused on the First Amendment rights of adults in determining the constitutionality of those regulations.

> *"The action of the local authorities in compelling the flag salute and pledge transcends constitutional limits of their power."*

# Students Have a First Amendment Right to Abstain from the Pledge of Allegiance

## The Supreme Court's Decision

### *Robert H. Jackson*

*In the following viewpoint Justice Robert H. Jackson, writing for the majority of the US Supreme Court, argues that the First Amendment of the US Constitution prohibits states from forcing students to salute the flag and recite the Pledge of Allegiance. Although the students who brought the case did so on the grounds that the West Virginia statute requiring them to salute the flag was against their religion, the Court ultimately made its decision purely on the basis of freedom of expression, regardless of a person's religion. Since the Court's decision, schools may lead students in the pledge of allegiance but must allow students the freedom to abstain from participating. Jackson was associate justice of the US Supreme Court from 1941 to 1954.*

The [West Virginia State] Board of Education on January 9, 1942, adopted a resolution . . . ordering that the salute to the flag become "a regular part of the program of activities in the public schools," that all teachers and pupils

> shall be required to participate in the salute honoring the Nation represented by the Flag; provided, however, that refusal to salute the Flag be regarded as an act of insubordination, and shall be dealt with accordingly.

The resolution originally required the "commonly accepted salute to the Flag," which it defined. Objections to the salute as "being too much like Hitler's" were raised by the Parent and Teacher Association, the Boy [Scouts] and Girl Scouts, the Red Cross, and the Federation of Women's Clubs. Some modification appears to have been made in deference to these objections, but no concession was made to Jehovah's Witnesses. What is now required is the "stiff-arm" salute, the saluter to keep the right hand raised with palm turned up while the following is repeated:

> I pledge allegiance to the Flag of the United States of America and to the republic for which it stands; one Nation, indivisible, with liberty and justice for all.

Failure to conform is "insubordination," dealt with by expulsion. Readmission is denied by statute until compliance. Meanwhile, the expelled child is "unlawfully absent," and may be proceeded against as a delinquent. His parents or guardians are liable to prosecution, and, if convicted, are subject to fine not exceeding $50 and Jail term not exceeding thirty days.

## Objection to the Mandatory Pledge

Appellees, citizens of the United States and of West Virginia, brought suit in the United States District Court for themselves and others similarly situated asking its injunction to restrain enforcement of these laws and regulations against Jehovah's Witnesses. The Witnesses are an unincorporated body teaching that the obligation imposed by law of God is superior to that of laws enacted by temporal government. Their religious beliefs include a literal version of Exodus, Chapter 20, verses 4 and 5, which says:

> Thou shalt not make unto thee any graven image, or any likeness of anything that is in heaven above, or that is in the earth beneath, or that is in the water under the earth; thou shalt not bow down thyself to them nor serve them.

They consider that the flag is an "image" within this command. For this reason, they refuse to salute it.

Children of this faith have been expelled from school and are threatened with exclusion for no other cause. Officials threaten to send them to reformatories maintained for criminally inclined juveniles. Parents of such children have been prosecuted, and are threatened with prosecutions for causing delinquency.

The Board of Education moved to dismiss the complaint, setting forth these facts and alleging that the law and regulations are an unconstitutional denial of religious freedom, and of freedom of speech, and are invalid under the "due process" and "equal protection" clauses of the Fourteenth Amendment to the Federal Constitution. The cause was submitted on the pleadings to a District Court of three judges. It restrained enforcement as to the plaintiffs and those of that class. The Board of Education brought the case here by direct appeal. . . .

The freedom asserted by these appellees does not bring them into collision with rights asserted by any other individual. It is such conflicts which most frequently require intervention of the State to determine where the rights of one end and those of another begin. But the refusal of these persons to participate in the ceremony does not interfere with or deny rights of others to do so. Nor is there any question in this case that their behavior is peaceable and orderly. The sole conflict is between authority and rights of the individual. The State asserts power to condition access to public education on making a prescribed sign and

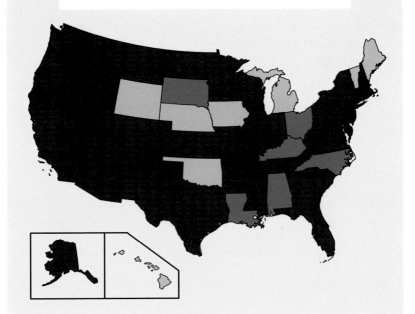

**PLEDGE OF ALLEGIANCE REQUIREMENTS FOR SCHOOLS, BY STATE**

According to an August 2003 report by the Education Commission of the States, state laws vary on whether schools are required to lead students in the Pledge of Allegiance.

Schools Required to Lead Students in the Pledge

Schools Have Option to Lead Students in the Pledge

No Law on the Pledge

Taken from: "State Requirements on Pledge of Allegiance in Schools," October 24, 2008, ProCon.org.

profession and at the same time to coerce attendance by punishing both parent and child. The latter stand on a right of self-determination in matters that touch individual opinion and personal attitude.

## The Compulsory Salute

As the present CHIEF JUSTICE said in dissent in the [*Minersville School District v.*] *Gobitis* [1940] case, the State may

> require teaching by instruction and study of all in our history and in the structure and organization of our government, including the guaranties of civil liberty, which tend to inspire patriotism and love of country.

Here, however, we are dealing with a compulsion of students to declare a belief. They are not merely made acquainted with the flag salute so that they may be informed as to what it is or even what it means. The issue here is whether this slow and easily neglected route to aroused loyalties constitutionally may be short-cut by substituting a compulsory salute and slogan. . . .

There is no doubt that, in connection with the pledges, the flag salute is a form of utterance. Symbolism is a primitive but effective way of communicating ideas. The use of an emblem or flag to symbolize some system, idea, institution, or personality is a short-cut from mind to mind. Causes and nations, political parties, lodges, and ecclesiastical groups seek to knit the loyalty of their followings to a flag or banner, a color or design. The State announces rank, function, and authority through crowns and maces, uniforms and black robes; the church speaks through the Cross, the Crucifix, the altar and shrine, and clerical raiment. Symbols of State often convey political ideas, just as religious symbols come to convey theological ones. Associated with many of these symbols are appropriate gestures of acceptance or respect: a salute, a bowed or bared head, a bended knee. A person gets from a symbol the meaning he puts into it, and what is one man's comfort and inspiration is another's jest and scorn.

Over a decade ago, Chief Justice [Charles Evans] Hughes led this Court in holding that the display of a red flag as a symbol of opposition by peaceful and legal means to organized government was protected by the free speech guaranties of the Constitution. Here, it is the State that employs a flag as a symbol of adherence to government as presently organized. It requires the individual to communicate by word and sign his acceptance of the political ideas it thus bespeaks. Objection to this form of communication, when coerced, is an old one, well known to the framers of the Bill of Rights.

## Forcing Expression of a Belief

It is also to be noted that the compulsory flag salute and pledge requires affirmation of a belief and an attitude of mind. It is not clear whether the regulation contemplates that pupils forgo any contrary convictions of their own and become unwilling converts to the prescribed ceremony, or whether it will be acceptable if they simulate assent by words without belief, and by a gesture barren of meaning. It is now a commonplace that censorship or suppression of expression of opinion is tolerated by our Constitution only when the expression presents a clear and present danger of action of a kind the State is empowered to prevent and punish. It would seem that involuntary affirmation could be commanded only on even more immediate and urgent grounds than silence. But here, the power of compulsion is invoked without any allegation that remaining passive during a flag salute ritual creates a clear and present danger that would justify an effort even to muffle expression. To sustain the compulsory flag salute, we are required to say that a Bill of Rights, which guards the individual's right to speak his own mind, left it open to public authorities to compel him to utter what is not in his mind.

Whether the First Amendment to the Constitution will permit officials to order observance of ritual of this nature does not depend upon whether as a voluntary exercise we would think it to be good, bad or merely innocuous. Any credo of nationalism is likely to include what some disapprove or to omit what others think essential, and to give off different overtones as it takes on different accents or interpretations. If official power exists to coerce acceptance of any patriotic creed, what it shall contain cannot be decided by courts but must be largely discretionary with the ordaining authority, whose power to prescribe would no doubt include power to amend. Hence, validity of the asserted power to force an American citizen publicly to profess any statement of belief, or to engage in any ceremony of assent to one, presents questions of power that must be considered independently of any idea we may have as to the utility of the ceremony in question.

Nor does the issue, as we see it, turn on one's possession of particular religious views or the sincerity with which they are held. While religion supplies appellees' motive for enduring the discomforts of making the issue in this case, many citizens who do not share these religious views hold such a compulsory rite to infringe constitutional liberty of the individual. It is not necessary to inquire whether nonconformist beliefs will exempt from the duty to salute unless we first find power to make the salute a legal duty. . . .

## The Authority of Education Boards

The Fourteenth Amendment, as now applied to the States, protects the citizen against the State itself and all of its creatures—Boards of Education not excepted. These have, of course, important, delicate, and highly discretionary functions, but none that they may not perform within the limits of the Bill of Rights. That they are educating the young for citizenship is reason for scrupulous protection of Constitutional freedoms of the individual, if we are not to strangle the free mind at its source and teach youth to discount important principles of our government as mere platitudes.

Such Boards are numerous, and their territorial jurisdiction often small. But small and local authority may feel less sense of responsibility to the Constitution, and agencies of publicity may be less vigilant in calling it to account. The action of Congress in making flag observance voluntary and respecting the conscience of the objector in a matter so vital as raising the Army contrasts sharply with these local regulations in matters relatively trivial to

*Students in Vincennes, In., salute the US flag. The US Supreme Court ruled that a student could not be compelled to salute the flag against his or her will.* © Linda Davidson/The Washington Post/Getty Images.

the welfare of the nation. There are village tyrants, as well as village Hampdens [courageous protesters], but none who acts under color of law [that is, under the appearance of or claim to legal authority or right] is beyond reach of the Constitution. . . .

## The Purpose of the First Amendment

Struggles to coerce uniformity of sentiment in support of some end thought essential to their time and country have been waged by many good, as well as by evil, men. Nationalism is a relatively recent phenomenon, but, at other times and places, the ends have been racial or territorial security, support of a dynasty or regime, and particular plans for saving souls. As first and moderate methods to attain unity have failed, those bent on its accomplishment must resort to an ever-increasing severity. As governmental pressure toward unity becomes greater, so strife becomes more bitter as to whose unity it shall be. Probably no deeper division of our people could proceed from any provocation than from finding it necessary to choose what doctrine and whose program public educational officials shall compel youth to unite in embracing. Ultimate futility of such attempts to compel coherence [uniformity of thought or behavior] is the lesson of every such effort from the [ancient] Roman drive to stamp out Christianity as a disturber of its pagan unity, the Inquisition, as a means to religious and dynastic unity, the Siberian exiles as a means to [Soviet] Russian unity, down to the fast-failing efforts of our present totalitarian enemies. Those who begin coercive elimination of dissent soon find themselves exterminating dissenters. Compulsory unification of opinion achieves only the unanimity [togetherness] of the graveyard.

It seems trite but necessary to say that the First Amendment to our Constitution was designed to avoid these ends by avoiding these beginnings. There is no mysticism in the American concept of the State or of the nature or origin of its authority. We set up government by consent of the governed, and the Bill of Rights denies those in power any legal opportunity to coerce that consent. Authority here is to be controlled by public opinion, not public opinion by authority.

The case is made difficult not because the principles of its decision are obscure, but because the flag involved is our own. Nevertheless, we apply the limitations of the Constitution with no fear that freedom to be intellectually and spiritually diverse or even contrary will disintegrate [tear apart] the social organization. To believe that patriotism will not flourish if patriotic ceremonies are voluntary and spontaneous, instead of a compulsory routine, is to make an unflattering estimate of the appeal of our institutions to free minds. We can have intellectual individualism and the rich cultural diversities that we owe to exceptional minds only at the price of occasional eccentricity and abnormal attitudes. When they are so harmless to others or to the State as those we deal with here, the price is not too great. But freedom to differ is not limited to things that do not matter much. That would be a mere shadow of freedom. The test of its substance is the right to differ as to things that touch the heart of the existing order.

If there is any fixed star in our constitutional constellation [that is, any guiding principle among our founding principles], it is that no official, high or petty, can prescribe what shall be orthodox in poetics, nationalism, religion, or other matters of opinion, or force citizens to confess by word or act their faith therein. If there are any circumstances which permit an exception, they do not now occur to us.

We think the action of the local authorities in compelling the flag salute and pledge transcends constitutional limitations on their power, and invades the sphere of intellect and spirit which it is the purpose of the First Amendment to our Constitution to reserve from all official control.

*"In our system, undifferentiated fear or apprehension of disturbance is not enough to overcome the right to freedom of expression."*

# Students Have a Right to Free Expression When It Does Not Cause Disruption

## The Supreme Court's Decision

### Abe Fortas

*In the following viewpoint Justice Abe Fortas, writing for the majority of the US Supreme Court, concludes that public schools may not limit student expression unless it substantially interferes with the operation of the school. In this case, the Court determined that it was unconstitutional for the Iowa schools to suspend three students who wore black armbands to school to protest the Vietnam War. The Court's decision in* Tinker *is frequently cited, though the Court continues to add to its understanding of what forms of student expression constitute a material disruption large enough that school officials may limit such expression without violating the First Amendment of the US Constitution. Fortas was associate*

Abe Fortas, Majority opinion, *Tinker v. Des Moines Independent Community School District*, US Supreme Court, February 24, 1969. Copyright © 1969 The Supreme Court of the United States.

*justice of the Court from 1965 to 1969, and he resigned from the Court in response to public controversy.*

Petitioner John F. Tinker, 15 years old, and petitioner Christopher Eckhardt, 16 years old, attended high schools in Des Moines, Iowa. Petitioner Mary Beth Tinker, John's sister, was a 13-year-old student in junior high school.

## The Suspended Students

In December 1965, a group of adults and students in Des Moines held a meeting at the Eckhardt home. The group determined to publicize their objections to the hostilities in Vietnam and their support for a truce by wearing black armbands during the holiday season and by fasting on December 16 and New Year's Eve [1965]. Petitioners and their parents had previously engaged in similar activities, and they decided to participate in the program.

The principals of the Des Moines schools became aware of the plan to wear armbands. On December 14, 1965, they met and adopted a policy that any student wearing an armband to school would be asked to remove it, and, if he refused, he would be suspended until he returned without the armband. Petitioners were aware of the regulation that the school authorities adopted.

On December 16 [1965], Mary Beth and Christopher wore black armbands to their schools. John Tinker wore his armband the next day [December 17, 1965]. They were all sent home and suspended from school until they would come back without their armbands. They did not return to school until after the planned period for wearing armbands had expired—that is, until after New Year's Day [1966].

This complaint was filed in the United States District Court by petitioners, through their fathers, under § 1983 of Title 42 of the United States Code. [The complaint demanded] an injunction restraining the respondent school officials and the respondent members of the board of directors of the school district from disciplining the petitioners, and it sought nominal damages. After an evidentiary hearing, the District Court dismissed the complaint. It upheld the constitutionality of the school authorities' action on the ground that it was reasonable in order to prevent disturbance of school discipline. The court referred to, but expressly declined to follow, the Fifth Circuit's holding in a similar case that the wearing of symbols like the armbands cannot be prohibited unless it "materially and substantially interfere[s] with the requirements of appropriate discipline in the operation of the school" [*Burnside v. Byars* (1966)].

On appeal, the Court of Appeals for the Eighth Circuit considered the case en banc [with all the judges of the court hearing the case, rather than a smaller panel of judges]. The court was equally divided, and the District Court's decision was accordingly affirmed without opinion. . . .

## Student Rights Versus School Rules

The District Court recognized that the wearing of an armband for the purpose of expressing certain views is the type of symbolic act that is within the Free Speech Clause of the First Amendment. As we shall discuss, the wearing of armbands in the circumstances of this case was entirely divorced from actually or potentially disruptive conduct by those participating in it. It was closely akin to "pure speech," which, we have repeatedly held, is entitled to comprehensive protection under the First Amendment.

First Amendment rights, applied in light of the special characteristics of the school environment, are available to teachers and students. It can hardly be argued that either students or teachers shed their constitutional rights to freedom of speech or expression at the schoolhouse gate. This has been the unmistakable holding of this Court for almost 50 years. In *Meyer v. Nebraska* (1923), and *Bartels v. Iowa* (1923), this Court, in opinions by Mr. Justice [James Clark] McReynolds, held that the Due Process Clause of the Fourteenth Amendment prevents States from forbidding the teaching of a foreign language to young students. Statutes to this effect, the Court held, unconstitutionally interfere with the liberty of teacher, student, and parent.

In *West Virginia v. Barnette* [1943] this Court held that, under the First Amendment, the student in public school may not be compelled to salute the flag. Speaking through Mr. Justice [Robert H.] Jackson, the Court said:

> The Fourteenth Amendment, as now applied to the States, protects the citizen against the State itself and all of its creatures—Boards of Education not excepted. These have, of course, important, delicate, and highly discretionary functions, but none that they may not perform within the limits of the Bill of Rights. That they are educating the young for citizenship is reason for scrupulous protection of Constitutional freedoms of the individual, if we are not to strangle the free mind at its source and teach youth to discount important principles of our government as mere platitudes.

On the other hand, the Court has repeatedly emphasized the need for affirming the comprehensive authority of the States and of school officials, consistent with fundamental constitutional safeguards, to prescribe and control conduct in the schools. Our problem lies in the area where students in the exercise of First Amendment rights collide with the rules of the school authorities.

## Passive Expression Without Disturbance

The problem posed by the present case does not relate to regulation of the length of skirts or the type of clothing, to hair style, or deportment. It does not concern aggressive, disruptive action or even group demonstrations. Our problem involves direct, primary First Amendment rights akin to "pure speech."

The school officials banned and sought to punish petitioners for a silent, passive expression of opinion, unaccompanied by any disorder or disturbance on the part of petitioners. There is here no evidence whatever of petitioners' interference, actual or nascent, with the schools' work or of collision with the rights of other students to be secure and to be let alone. Accordingly, this case does not concern speech or action that intrudes upon the work of the schools or the rights of other students.

Only a few of the 18,000 students in the school system wore the black armbands. Only five students were suspended for wearing them. There is no indication that the work of the schools or any class was disrupted. Outside the classrooms, a few students made hostile remarks to the children wearing armbands, but there were no threats or acts of violence on school premises.

The District Court concluded that the action of the school authorities was reasonable because it was based upon their fear of a disturbance from the wearing of the armbands. But, in our system, undifferentiated fear or apprehension of disturbance is not enough to overcome the right to freedom of expression. Any departure from absolute regimentation may cause trouble. Any variation from the majority's opinion may inspire fear. Any word spoken, in class, in the lunchroom, or on the campus, that deviates from the views of another person may start an argument or cause a disturbance. But our Constitution says we must take this risk, and our history says that it is this sort of hazardous freedom—this kind of openness—that is the basis of our national strength and of the independence and vigor of Americans who grow up and live in this relatively permissive, often disputatious, society.

In order for the State in the person of school officials to justify prohibition of a particular expression of opinion, it must be able to show that its action was caused by something more than a mere desire to avoid the discomfort and unpleasantness that always accompany an unpopular viewpoint. Certainly where there is no finding and no showing that engaging in the forbidden conduct would "materially and substantially interfere with the requirements of appropriate discipline in the operation of the school," the prohibition cannot be sustained.

In the present case, the District Court made no such finding, and our independent examination of the record fails to yield evidence that the school authorities had reason to anticipate that the wearing of the armbands would substantially interfere with the work of the school or impinge upon the rights of other students. Even an official memorandum prepared after the suspension that listed the reasons for the ban on wearing the armbands made no reference to the anticipation of such disruption.

## The Actions of School Officials

On the contrary, the action of the school authorities appears to have been based upon an urgent wish to avoid the controversy which might result from the expression, even by the silent symbol of armbands, of opposition to this Nation's part in the conflagration in Vietnam.

It is revealing, in this respect, that the meeting at which the school principals decided to issue the contested regulation was

*Mary Beth and John Tinker show their black armbands worn in protest against the Vietnam War. The US Supreme Court ruled that they had a First Amendment right to wear the armbands to school.* © Bettmann/Corbis.

called in response to a student's statement to the journalism teacher in one of the schools that he wanted to write an article on Vietnam and have it published in the school paper. (The student was dissuaded.)

It is also relevant that the school authorities did not purport to prohibit the wearing of all symbols of political or controversial significance. The record shows that students in some of the schools wore buttons relating to national political campaigns, and some even wore the Iron Cross, traditionally a symbol of Nazism.

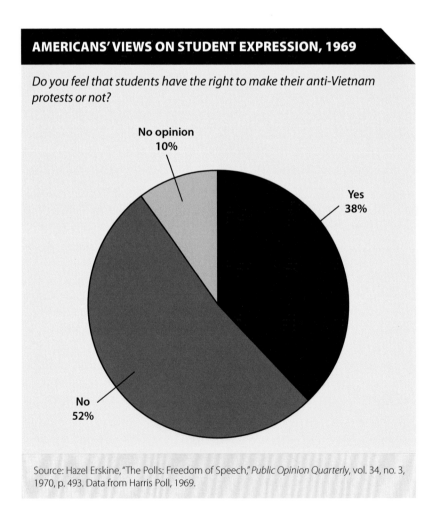

**AMERICANS' VIEWS ON STUDENT EXPRESSION, 1969**

*Do you feel that students have the right to make their anti-Vietnam protests or not?*

No opinion
10%

Yes
38%

No
52%

Source: Hazel Erskine, "The Polls: Freedom of Speech," *Public Opinion Quarterly*, vol. 34, no. 3, 1970, p. 493. Data from Harris Poll, 1969.

The order prohibiting the wearing of armbands did not extend to these. Instead, a particular symbol—black armbands worn to exhibit opposition to this Nation's involvement in Vietnam—was singled out for prohibition. Clearly, the prohibition of expression of one particular opinion, at least without evidence that it is necessary to avoid material and substantial interference with schoolwork or discipline, is not constitutionally permissible.

In our system, state-operated schools [are not allowed to] be enclaves of totalitarianism. School officials do not possess absolute authority over their students. Students in school, as well as out of school, are "persons" under our Constitution. They are possessed of fundamental rights which the State must respect, just as they themselves must respect their obligations to the State. In our system, students may not be regarded as closed-circuit recipients of only that which the State chooses to communicate. They may not be confined to the expression of those sentiments that are officially approved. In the absence of a specific showing of constitutionally valid reasons to regulate their speech, students are entitled to freedom of expression of their views. As Judge [Walter] Gewin, speaking for the Fifth Circuit, said, school officials cannot suppress "expressions of feelings with which they do not wish to contend."

## Freedom of Student Speech

In *Meyer*, Mr. Justice McReynolds expressed this Nation's repudiation of the principle that a State might so conduct its schools as to "foster a homogeneous people." He said:

> In order to submerge the individual and develop ideal citizens, Sparta assembled the males at seven into barracks and entrusted their subsequent education and training to official guardians. Although such measures have been deliberately approved by men of great genius, their ideas touching the relation between individual and State were wholly different from those upon which our institutions rest; and it hardly will be affirmed that any legislature could impose such restrictions

upon the people of a State without doing violence to both letter and spirit of the Constitution.

This principle has been repeated by this Court on numerous occasions during the intervening years. In *Keyishian v. Board
of Regents* [1967], MR. JUSTICE BRENNAN, speaking for the
Court, said:

> "The vigilant protection of constitutional freedoms is no-
> where more vital than in the community of American schools"
> *Shelton v. Tucker* [1960]. The classroom is peculiarly the "mar-
> ketplace of ideas." The Nation's future depends upon leaders
> trained through wide exposure to that robust exchange of ideas
> which discovers truth "out of a multitude of tongues, [rather]
> than through any kind of authoritative selection."

The principle of these cases is not confined to the supervised
and ordained discussion which takes place in the classroom. The
principal use to which the schools are dedicated is to accommo-
date students during prescribed hours for the purpose of certain
types of activities. Among those activities is personal intercom-
munication among the students. This is not only an inevitable
part of the process of attending school; it is also an important
part of the educational process. A student's rights, therefore, do
not embrace merely the classroom hours. When he is in the cafeteria, or on the playing field, or on the campus during the authorized hours, he may express his opinions, even on controversial
subjects like the conflict in Vietnam, if he does so without "materially and substantially interfer[ing] with the requirements of appropriate discipline in the operation of the school" and without
colliding with the rights of others. But conduct by the student, in
class or out of it, which for any reason—whether it stems from
time, place, or type of behavior—materially disrupts classwork
or involves substantial disorder or invasion of the rights of others
is, of course, not immunized by the constitutional guarantee of
freedom of speech.

# Limits on Free Expression

Under our Constitution, free speech is not a right that is given only to be so circumscribed that it exists in principle, but not in fact. Freedom of expression would not truly exist if the right could be exercised only in an area that a benevolent government has provided as a safe haven for crackpots. The Constitution says that Congress (and the States) may not abridge the right to free speech. This provision means what it says. We properly read it to permit reasonable regulation of speech-connected activities in carefully restricted circumstances. But we do not confine the permissible exercise of First Amendment rights to a telephone booth or the four corners of a pamphlet, or to supervised and ordained discussion in a school classroom.

If a regulation were adopted by school officials forbidding discussion of the Vietnam conflict, or the expression by any student of opposition to it anywhere on school property except as part of a prescribed classroom exercise, it would be obvious that the regulation would violate the constitutional rights of students, at least if it could not be justified by a showing that the students' activities would materially and substantially disrupt the work and discipline of the school. In the circumstances of the present case, the prohibition of the silent, passive "witness of the arm-bands," as one of the children called it, is no less offensive to the Constitution's guarantees.

As we have discussed, the record does not demonstrate any facts which might reasonably have led school authorities to forecast substantial disruption of or material interference with school activities, and no disturbances or disorders on the school premises in fact occurred. These petitioners merely went about their ordained rounds in school. Their deviation consisted only in wearing on their sleeve a band of black cloth, not more than two inches wide. They wore it to exhibit their disapproval of the Vietnam hostilities and their advocacy of a truce, to make their views known, and, by their example, to influence others to adopt them. They neither interrupted school activities nor sought to intrude in the school affairs or the lives of others. They caused discussion outside of the classrooms, but no interference with work and no disorder. In the circumstances, our Constitution does not permit officials of the State to deny their form of expression.

> "The First Amendment does not prevent
> ... determining that to permit a vulgar
> and lewd speech ... would undermine
> the school's basic educational mission."

# Schools Can Limit Vulgar Student Speech

## The Supreme Court's Decision

### Warren E. Burger

*In the following viewpoint Chief Justice Warren E. Burger, writing for the majority of the Court, argued that the First Amendment rights of students to free expression may be limited by school officials when that expression is sexually vulgar. In coming to this decision, the Court disagreed with the lower court rulings, which had determined that Matthew N. Fraser's sexually explicit speech was protected in the same manner as political speech. The Court concluded that encouraging socially appropriate behavior and protecting children from sexually explicit language are legitimate goals of public schools that permit school officials to limit vulgar student speech that may thwart these goals. Burger was chief justice of the US Supreme Court from 1969 until his retirement in 1986.*

On April 26, 1983, respondent Matthew N. Fraser, a student at Bethel High School in Pierce County, Washington, delivered a speech nominating a fellow student for student elective office. Approximately 600 high school students, many of whom were 14-year-olds, attended the assembly. Students were required to attend the assembly or to report to the study hall. The assembly was part of a school-sponsored educational program in self-government. Students who elected not to attend the assembly were required to report to study hall. During the entire speech, Fraser referred to his candidate in terms of an elaborate, graphic, and explicit sexual metaphor.

## Suspension for Obscene Speech

Two of Fraser's teachers, with whom he discussed the contents of his speech in advance, informed him that the speech was "inappropriate and that he probably should not deliver it," and that his delivery of the speech might have "severe consequences."

During Fraser's delivery of the speech, a school counselor observed the reaction of students to the speech. Some students hooted and yelled; some by gestures graphically simulated the sexual activities pointedly alluded to in respondent's speech. Other students appeared to be bewildered and embarrassed by the speech. One teacher reported that, on the day following the speech, she found it necessary to forgo a portion of the scheduled class lesson in order to discuss the speech with the class.

A Bethel High School disciplinary rule prohibiting the use of obscene language in the school provides:

> Conduct which materially and substantially interferes with the educational process is prohibited, including the use of obscene, profane language or gestures.

The morning after the assembly, the Assistant Principal called Fraser into her office and notified him that the school considered his speech to have been a violation of this rule. Fraser was presented with copies of five letters submitted by teachers, describing his conduct at the assembly; he was given a chance to explain his conduct and he admitted to having given the speech described and that he deliberately used sexual innuendo in the speech. Fraser was then informed that he would be suspended for three days, and that his name would be removed from the list of candidates for graduation speaker at the school's commencement exercises.

Fraser sought review of this disciplinary action through the School District's grievance procedures. The hearing officer determined that the speech given by respondent was "indecent, lewd, and offensive to the modesty and decency of many of the students and faculty in attendance at the assembly." The examiner determined that the speech fell within the ordinary meaning of "obscene," as used in the disruptive conduct rule, and affirmed the discipline in its entirety. Fraser served two days of his suspension, and was allowed to return to school on the third day.

## The Lower Court Decisions

Respondent, by his father as guardian *ad litem* [for the lawsuit], then brought this action in the United States District Court for the Western District of Washington. Respondent alleged a violation of his First Amendment right to freedom of speech, and sought both injunctive relief and monetary damages under 42 U.S.C. § 1983. The District Court held that the school's sanctions violated respondent's right to freedom of speech under the First Amendment to the United States Constitution, that the school's disruptive conduct rule is unconstitutionally vague and overbroad, and that the removal of respondent's name from the graduation speaker's list violated the Due Process Clause of the Fourteenth Amendment because the disciplinary rule makes no mention of such removal as a possible sanction. The District Court awarded respondent $278 in damages, $12,750 in litigation costs and attorney's fees, and enjoined the School District from preventing respondent from speaking at the commencement ceremonies. Respondent, who had been elected graduation speaker by a write-in vote of his classmates, delivered a speech at the commencement ceremonies on June 8, 1983.

The Court of Appeals for the Ninth Circuit affirmed the judgment of the District Court, holding that respondent's speech was indistinguishable from the protest armband in *Tinker v. Des Moines Independent Community School Dist.* (1969). The court explicitly rejected the School District's argument that the speech, unlike the passive conduct of wearing a black armband, had a disruptive effect on the educational process. The Court of Appeals also rejected the School District's argument that it had an interest in protecting an essentially captive audience of minors from lewd and indecent language in a setting sponsored by the school, reasoning that the School District's "unbridled discretion" to determine what discourse is "decent" would "increase the risk of cementing white, middle-class standards for determining what is acceptable and proper speech and behavior in our public schools." Finally, the Court of Appeals rejected the School District's argument that, incident to its responsibility for the school curriculum, it had the power to control the language used to express ideas during a school-sponsored activity. . . .

## The Difference Between Political and Sexual Speech

This Court acknowledged in *Tinker* that students do not "shed their constitutional rights to freedom of speech or expression at the schoolhouse gate." The Court of Appeals read that case as precluding any discipline of Fraser for indecent speech and lewd conduct in the school assembly. That court appears to have proceeded on the theory that the use of lewd and obscene speech in order to make what the speaker considered to be a point in a nominating speech for a fellow student was essentially the same as the wearing of an armband in *Tinker* as a form of protest or the expression of a political position.

The marked distinction between the political "message" of the armbands in *Tinker* and the sexual content of respondent's speech in this case seems to have been given little weight by the Court of Appeals. In upholding the students' right to engage in a nondisruptive, passive expression of a political viewpoint in *Tinker*, this Court was careful to note that the case did "not concern speech or action that intrudes upon the work of the schools or the rights of other students."

It is against this background that we turn to consider the level of First Amendment protection accorded to Fraser's utterances and actions before an official high school assembly attended by 600 students.

## The Fundamental Values of Democratic Society

The role and purpose of the American public school system were well described by two historians [C. Beard and M. Beard] who stated:

> [P]ublic education must prepare pupils for citizenship in the Republic. . . . It must inculcate the habits and manners of civility as values in themselves conducive to happiness and as indispensable to the practice of self-government in the community and the nation.

In *Ambach v. Norwick* (1979), we echoed the essence of this statement of the objectives of public education as the "inculcat[ion of] fundamental values necessary to the maintenance of a democratic political system."

These fundamental values of "habits and manners of civility" essential to a democratic society must, of course, include tolerance of divergent political and religious views, even when the views expressed may be unpopular. But these "fundamental values" must also take into account consideration of the sensibilities of others, and, in the case of a school, the sensibilities of fellow students. The undoubted freedom to advocate unpopular and controversial views in schools and classrooms must be balanced against the society's countervailing interest in teaching students

*Matthew Fraser stands in front of Bethel Senior High School. The US Supreme Court ruled that his sexually explicit speech was different from political speech and therefore was not protected by the First Amendment.* © Bettmann/Corbis.

the boundaries of socially appropriate behavior. Even the most heated political discourse in a democratic society requires consideration for the personal sensibilities of the other participants and audiences.

In our Nation's legislative halls, where some of the most vigorous political debates in our society are carried on, there are rules prohibiting the use of expressions offensive to other participants in the debate. The Manual of Parliamentary Practice, drafted by Thomas Jefferson and adopted by the House of Representatives to govern the proceedings in that body, prohibits the use of "impertinent" speech during debate, and likewise provides that "[n]o person is to use indecent language against the proceedings

## STUDENT VIEWS OF CENSORSHIP

*Please indicate whether or not you think each of the following steps is an appropriate measure for public schools to take.*

■ Yes    □ No

**Restricting foul (bad) language in writing assignments**

75%

25%

**Placing limits on what students can write about in the school newspaper**

45%

55%

**Banning books, newspapers, and magazines considered by school officials to be offensive**

44%

56%

Asked of US teens ages 13–17.

Taken from: Julie Ray, "Censorship: Do Teens Bow to School Control?" Gallup, July 12, 2005. www.gallup.com.

of the House." The Rules of Debate applicable in the Senate likewise provide that a Senator may be called to order for imputing improper motives to another Senator or for referring offensively to any state. Senators have been censured for abusive language directed at other Senators. Can it be that what is proscribed in the halls of Congress is beyond the reach of school officials to regulate?

## Offensive Speech in Public School

The First Amendment guarantees wide freedom in matters of adult public discourse. A sharply divided Court upheld the right to express an antidraft viewpoint in a public place, albeit in terms highly offensive to most citizens. It does not follow, however, that, simply because the use of an offensive form of expression may not be prohibited to adults making what the speaker considers a political point, the same latitude must be permitted to children in a public school. In *New Jersey v. T.L.O.* (1985), we reaffirmed that the constitutional rights of students in public school are not automatically coextensive with the rights of adults in other settings. . . .

Surely it is a highly appropriate function of public school education to prohibit the use of vulgar and offensive terms in public discourse. Indeed, the "fundamental values necessary to the maintenance of a democratic political system" disfavor the use of terms of debate highly offensive or highly threatening to others. Nothing in the Constitution prohibits the states from insisting that certain modes of expression are inappropriate and subject to sanctions. The inculcation of these values is truly the "work of the schools." The determination of what manner of speech in the classroom or in school assembly is inappropriate properly rests with the school board.

The process of educating our youth for citizenship in public schools is not confined to books, the curriculum, and the civics class; schools must teach by example the shared values of a civilized social order. Consciously or otherwise, teachers—and indeed the older students—demonstrate the appropriate form of civil discourse and political expression by their conduct and deportment in and out of class. Inescapably, like parents, they are role models. The schools, as instruments of the state, may determine that the essential lessons of civil, mature conduct cannot be conveyed in a school that tolerates lewd, indecent, or offensive speech and conduct such as that indulged in by this confused boy.

The pervasive sexual innuendo in Fraser's speech was plainly offensive to both teachers and students—indeed, to any mature person. By glorifying male sexuality, and in its verbal content, the speech was acutely insulting to teenage girl students. The speech could well be seriously damaging to its less mature audience, many of whom were only 14 years old and on the threshold of awareness of human sexuality. Some students were reported as bewildered by the speech and the reaction of mimicry it provoked.

## The Limitations of the First Amendment

This Court's First Amendment jurisprudence has acknowledged limitations on the otherwise absolute interest of the speaker in reaching an unlimited audience where the speech is sexually explicit and the audience may include children. In *Ginsberg v. New York* (1968), this Court upheld a New York statute banning the sale of sexually oriented material to minors, even though the material in question was entitled to First Amendment protection with respect to adults. And in addressing the question whether the First Amendment places any limit on the authority of public schools to remove books from a public school library, all Members of the Court, otherwise sharply divided, acknowledged that the school board has the authority to remove books that are vulgar. These cases recognize the obvious concern on the part of parents, and school authorities acting *in loco parentis* [in the place of a parent], to protect children especially in a captive audience—from exposure to sexually explicit, indecent, or lewd speech. . . .

We hold that petitioner School District acted entirely within its permissible authority in imposing sanctions upon Fraser in response to his offensively lewd and indecent speech. Unlike the sanctions imposed on the students wearing armbands in *Tinker*, the penalties imposed in this case were unrelated to any political viewpoint. The First Amendment does not prevent the school officials from determining that to permit a vulgar and lewd speech such as respondent's would undermine the school's basic educational mission. A high school assembly or classroom is no place for a sexually explicit monologue directed towards an unsuspecting audience of teenage students. Accordingly, it was perfectly appropriate for the school to disassociate itself to make the point to the pupils that vulgar speech and lewd conduct is wholly inconsistent with the "fundamental values" of public school education.

> *"We hold that educators do not offend the First Amendment by exercising editorial control over the style and content of student speech in school-sponsored expressive activities."*

# Schools Can Censor Student Speech in School Publications

## The Supreme Court's Decision

### Byron White

*In the following viewpoint Justice Byron White, writing for the majority of the Court, argues that student expression may be censored without violating the First Amendment when such speech is part of school-sponsored activities and such censorship is reasonably related to educational purposes. The Court makes a point of differentiating student expression in the school newspaper, as in this case, from student expression unrelated to school activities, such as the political speech of the students wearing armbands to protest the* Vietnam War *in* Tinker v. Des Moines Independent Community School District *(1969). In this case, the Court added to the realm of legitimately restricted student expression, further delineating the difference between the free expression rights of adults and those of students in public schools. White was associate justice of the US Supreme Court from 1962 until his retirement in 1993.*

Byron White, Majority opinion, *Hazelwood School District v. Kuhlmeier*, US Supreme Court, January 13, 1988. Copyright © 1988 The Supreme Court of the United States.

This case concerns the extent to which educators may exercise editorial control over the contents of a high school newspaper produced as part of the school's journalism curriculum.

## The Censored Student Newspaper

Petitioners are the Hazelwood School District in St. Louis County, Missouri; various school officials; Robert Eugene Reynolds, the principal of Hazelwood East High School; and Howard Emerson, a teacher in the school district. Respondents are three former Hazelwood East students who were staff members of *Spectrum*, the school newspaper. They contend that school officials violated their First Amendment rights by deleting two pages of articles from the May 13, 1983, issue of *Spectrum*.

*Spectrum* was written and edited by the Journalism II class at Hazelwood East. The newspaper was published every three weeks or so during the 1982–1983 school year. More than 4,500 copies of the newspaper were distributed during that year to students, school personnel, and members of the community.

The Board of Education allocated funds from its annual budget for the printing of *Spectrum*. These funds were supplemented by proceeds from sales of the newspaper. The printing expenses during the 1982–1983 school year totaled $4,668.50; revenue from sales was $1,166.84. The other costs associated with the newspaper—such as supplies, textbooks, and a portion of the journalism teacher's salary—were borne entirely by the Board.

The Journalism II course was taught by Robert Stergos for most of the 1982–1983 academic year. Stergos left Hazelwood East to take a job in private industry on April 29, 1983, when the May 13 edition of *Spectrum* was nearing completion, and petitioner Emerson took his place as newspaper adviser for the remaining weeks of the term.

The practice at Hazelwood East during the spring 1983 semester was for the journalism teacher to submit page proofs of each *Spectrum* issue to Principal Reynolds for his review prior to publication. On May 10 [1983], Emerson delivered the proofs of the May 13 edition to Reynolds, who objected to two of the articles scheduled to appear in that edition. One of the stories described three Hazelwood East students' experiences with pregnancy; the other discussed the impact of divorce on students at the school.

Reynolds was concerned that, although the pregnancy story used false names "to keep the identity of these girls a secret," the pregnant students still might be identifiable from the text. He

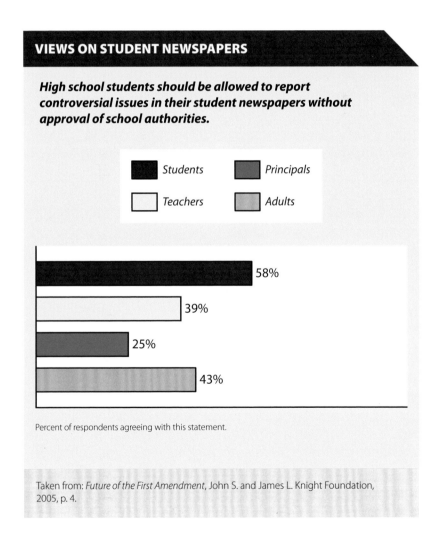

**VIEWS ON STUDENT NEWSPAPERS**

*High school students should be allowed to report controversial issues in their student newspapers without approval of school authorities.*

Students
Teachers
Principals
Adults

58%

39%

25%

43%

Percent of respondents agreeing with this statement.

Taken from: *Future of the First Amendment*, John S. and James L. Knight Foundation, 2005, p. 4.

also believed that the article's references to sexual activity and birth control were inappropriate for some of the younger students at the school. In addition, Reynolds was concerned that a student identified by name in the divorce story had complained that her father "wasn't spending enough time with my mom, my sister and I" prior to the divorce, "was always out of town on business or out late playing cards with the guys," and "always argued about everything" with her mother. Reynolds believed that the student's parents should have been given an opportunity to respond to these remarks, or to consent to their publication. He was unaware that Emerson had deleted the student's name from the final version of the article.

Reynolds believed that there was no time to make the necessary changes in the stories before the scheduled press run, and that the newspaper would not appear before the end of the school year if printing were delayed to any significant extent. He concluded that his only options under the circumstances were to publish a four-page newspaper instead of the planned six-page newspaper, eliminating the two pages on which the offending stories appeared, or to publish no newspaper at all. Accordingly, he directed Emerson to withhold from publication the two pages containing the stories on pregnancy and divorce. He informed his superiors of the decision, and they concurred. . . .

## Student Expression Is Subject to the School Board

Students in the public schools do not "shed their constitutional rights to freedom of speech or expression at the schoolhouse gate" [*Tinker v. Des Moines Independent Community* (1969)]. They cannot be punished merely for expressing their personal views on the school premises—whether "in the cafeteria, or on the playing field, or on the campus during the authorized hours"—unless school authorities have reason to believe that such expression will "substantially interfere with the work of the school or impinge upon the rights of other students."

We have nonetheless recognized that the First Amendment rights of students in the public schools "are not automatically co-extensive with the rights of adults in other settings" [*Bethel School District No. 403 v. Fraser* (1986)], and must be "applied in light of the special characteristics of the school environment." A school need not tolerate student speech that is inconsistent with its "basic educational mission," even though the government could not censor similar speech outside the school. Accordingly, we held in *Fraser* that a student could be disciplined for having delivered a speech that was "sexually explicit" but not legally obscene at an official school assembly, because the school was entitled to "disassociate itself" from the speech in a manner that would demonstrate to others that such vulgarity is "wholly inconsistent with the 'fundamental values' of public school education." We thus recognized that "[t]he determination of what manner of speech in the classroom or in school assembly is inappropriate properly

*School newspapers can be censored because they are a school-supported product and the public might reasonably conclude that the school has given its approval to the paper's content.* © Brian Branch Price/Bloomberg via Getty Images.

rests with the school board," rather than with the federal courts. It is in this context that respondents' First Amendment claims must be considered. . . .

## The Promotion of Student Speech

The question whether the First Amendment requires a school to tolerate particular student speech—the question that we addressed in *Tinker*—is different from the question whether the First Amendment requires a school affirmatively to promote particular student speech. The former question addresses educators' ability to silence a student's personal expression that happens to occur on the school premises. The latter question concerns educators' authority over school-sponsored publications, theatrical productions, and other expressive activities that students, parents, and members of the public might reasonably perceive to bear the imprimatur of the school. These activities may fairly be characterized as part of the school curriculum, whether or not they occur in a traditional classroom setting, so long as they are supervised by faculty members and designed to impart particular knowledge or skills to student participants and audiences.

Educators are entitled to exercise greater control over this second form of student expression to assure that participants learn whatever lessons the activity is designed to teach, that readers or listeners are not exposed to material that may be inappropriate for their level of maturity, and that the views of the individual speaker are not erroneously attributed to the school. Hence, a school may, in its capacity as publisher of a school newspaper or producer of a school play, "disassociate itself" [*Fraser*], not only from speech that would "substantially interfere with [its] work . . . or impinge upon the rights of other students" [*Tinker*], but also from speech that is, for example, ungrammatical, poorly written, inadequately researched, biased or prejudiced, vulgar or profane, or unsuitable for immature audiences. A school must be able to set high standards for the student speech that is disseminated under its auspices—standards that may be higher than those demanded by some newspaper publishers or theatrical producers in the "real" world—and may refuse to disseminate student speech that does not meet those standards. In addition, a school must be able to take into account the emotional maturity of the intended audience in determining whether to disseminate student speech on potentially sensitive topics, which might range from the existence of Santa Claus in an elementary school setting to the particulars of teenage sexual activity in a high school setting. A school must also retain the authority to refuse to sponsor student speech that might reasonably be perceived to advocate drug or alcohol use, irresponsible sex, or conduct otherwise inconsistent with "the shared values of a civilized social order" [*Fraser*], or to associate the school with any position other than neutrality on matters of political controversy. Otherwise, the schools would be unduly constrained from fulfilling their role as

> a principal instrument in awakening the child to cultural values, in preparing him for later professional training, and in helping him to adjust normally to his environment. [*Brown v. Board of Education* (1954)]

Accordingly, we conclude that the standard articulated in *Tinker* for determining when a school may punish student expression need not also be the standard for determining when a school may refuse to lend its name and resources to the dissemination of student expression. Instead, we hold that educators do not offend the First Amendment by exercising editorial control over the style and content of student speech in school-sponsored expressive activities, so long as their actions are reasonably related to legitimate pedagogical concerns.

This standard is consistent with our oft-expressed view that the education of the Nation's youth is primarily the responsibility of parents, teachers, and state and local school officials, and not of federal judges. It is only when the decision to censor a school-sponsored publication, theatrical production, or other vehicle of student expression has no valid educational purpose that the

First Amendment is so "directly and sharply implicate[d]," as to require judicial intervention to protect students' constitutional rights.

## A Reasonable Restriction of Student Expression

We also conclude that Principal Reynolds acted reasonably in requiring the deletion from the May 13 [1983] issue of *Spectrum* of the pregnancy article, the divorce article, and the remaining articles that were to appear on the same pages of the newspaper.

The initial paragraph of the pregnancy article declared that "[a]ll names have been changed to keep the identity of these girls a secret." The principal concluded that the students' anonymity was not adequately protected, however, given the other identifying information in the article and the small number of pregnant students at the school. Indeed, a teacher at the school credibly testified that she could positively identify at least one of the girls, and possibly all three. It is likely that many students at Hazelwood East would have been at least as successful in identifying the girls. Reynolds therefore could reasonably have feared that the article violated whatever pledge of anonymity had been given to the pregnant students. In addition, he could reasonably have been concerned that the article was not sufficiently sensitive to the privacy interests of the students' boyfriends and parents, who were discussed in the article but who were given no opportunity to consent to its publication or to offer a response. The article did not contain graphic accounts of sexual activity. The girls did comment in the article, however, concerning their sexual histories and their use or nonuse of birth control. It was not unreasonable for the principal to have concluded that such frank talk was inappropriate in a school-sponsored publication distributed to 14-year-old freshmen and presumably taken home to be read by students' even younger brothers and sisters.

The student who was quoted by name in the version of the divorce article seen by Principal Reynolds made comments sharply critical of her father. The principal could reasonably have concluded that an individual publicly identified as an inattentive parent—indeed, as one who chose "playing cards with the guys" over home and family—was entitled to an opportunity to defend himself as a matter of journalistic fairness. These concerns were shared by both of *Spectrum's* faculty advisers for the 1982–1983 school year, who testified that they would not have allowed the article to be printed without deletion of the student's name.

Principal Reynolds testified credibly at trial that, at the time that he reviewed the proofs of the May 13 [1983] issue during an extended telephone conversation with Emerson, he believed that there was no time to make any changes in the articles, and that the newspaper had to be printed immediately or not at all. It is true that Reynolds did not verify whether the necessary modifications could still have been made in the articles, and that Emerson did not volunteer the information that printing could be delayed until the changes were made. We nonetheless agree with the District Court that the decision to excise the two pages containing the problematic articles was reasonable, given the particular circumstances of this case. These circumstances included the very recent replacement of Stergos by Emerson, who may not have been entirely familiar with *Spectrum* editorial and production procedures, and the pressure felt by Reynolds to make an immediate decision so that students would not be deprived of the newspaper altogether.

In sum, we cannot reject as unreasonable Principal Reynolds' conclusion that neither the pregnancy article nor the divorce article was suitable for publication in *Spectrum*. Reynolds could reasonably have concluded that the students who had written and edited these articles had not sufficiently mastered those portions of the Journalism II curriculum that pertained to the treatment of controversial issues and personal attacks, the need to protect the privacy of individuals whose most intimate concerns are to be revealed in the newspaper, and "the legal, moral, and ethical restrictions imposed upon journalists within [a] school community" that includes adolescent subjects and readers. Finally, we conclude that the principal's decision to delete two pages of *Spectrum*, rather than to delete only the offending articles or to require that they be modified, was reasonable under the circumstances as he understood them. Accordingly, no violation of First Amendment rights occurred.

> "[The Court] found the university's action in confiscating the yearbooks a violation of the First Amendment."

# Speech Restrictions on High School Students Do Not Apply to College Students

## James Tidwell

*In the following viewpoint James Tidwell contends that the United States Court of Appeals for the Sixth Circuit's decision in* Kincaid v. Gibson *(2001) is good news for college students. Tidwell claims that the court in this decision drew a line between high school students and college students and found that restrictions to student expression that may be reasonable for high school do not apply in college, as students in college are adults. Although the issue of the case was whether college officials may censor a student yearbook, Tidwell claims that the reasoning of the case makes it unlikely that future court decisions will find any restrictions on college student expression—including that in the college newspaper—to be unconstitutional without a compelling interest. Tidwell is professor and chair of the Department of Journalism at Eastern Illinois University.*

It was a classic legal battle pitting the First Amendment rights of college student journalists against the authority of college administrators to control the content of campus media.

It was also an opportunity for a federal appellate court to decide whether a U.S. Supreme Court precedent involving high school journalists was applicable to college journalists.

## An Issue of College Student Expression

The case—*Kincaid v. Gibson* [2001]—came about after officials at Kentucky State University [KSU] confiscated and refused to distribute the university's student yearbook that covered the 1992–94 school years.

Betty Gibson, the vice president for student affairs at Kentucky State, thought the quality of the yearbook was poor and the content was inappropriate, according to court records. She objected to the yearbook's purple cover (not the school colors), its "destination unknown" theme, the lack of captions under many of the photos and the inclusion of current events ostensibly unrelated to KSU.

Two KSU students, Charles Kincaid and yearbook editor Capri Coffer, sued the university, alleging their rights under the First and 14th amendments had been violated.

In January [2001], the U.S. Court of Appeals for the 6th Circuit came down firmly on the side of the students. It also refused to equate the legal rights of college journalists with high school journalists. The 10–3 decision reversed a decision in favor of KSU by a federal district judge and a divided three-judge panel of the 6th Circuit.

## The Difference Between High School and College

A long series of precedents in both state and federal courts going back more than 30 years has established the First Amendment rights of student journalists in public universities and colleges.

But in the 1988 case of *Hazelwood v. Kuhlmeier*, the U.S. Supreme Court ruled that high school officials had broad power to regulate the content of student newspapers if their decisions were reasonably related to legitimate pedagogical concerns. Since then, legal observers had wondered whether the *Hazelwood* analysis was applicable to colleges. In fact, the *Kincaid* trial judge cited *Hazelwood* in ruling that KSU's actions were reasonable and did not violate the First Amendment.

The 6th Circuit majority in *Kincaid* made it clear that the context of this case—the fact that it occurred on a college campus—was different than *Hazelwood*. "The university is a special place for purposes of First Amendment jurisprudence," the Court said. Quoting the U.S. Supreme Court, the opinion noted that the danger of "chilling individual thought and expression is especially real in the university setting, where the state acts against a background and tradition of thought and experiment that is at the center of our intellectual and philosophic tradition."

The decision also noted that college students are adults and there was no justification for giving school officials greater control over the content of student media because the content might be "unsuitable for immature audiences," as was the case in *Hazelwood*.

## The Public Forum Doctrine

Another factor that makes this case important is the 6th Circuit's application of the "public forum" doctrine to college student media. None of the previous college cases used this approach. They were decided prior to the creation of the forum analysis by the U.S. Supreme Court in 1983.

The Supreme Court created the public forum analysis to determine appropriate government control of speech that takes place on or in property owned by the government.

The 6th Circuit found the KSU yearbook to be a designated public forum (sometimes referred to as a "limited public forum"). It was property that by policy and/or practice the government

*At the university level, a school must show a "compelling interest" before legitimately censoring its yearbook.* © AP Images/Terry Gilliam.

had opened up for speech and debate by the general public or by certain speakers. Government may control the content of speech in a designated public forum only if it has a compelling reason to do so.

Had the Court agreed with the district judge that the yearbook was a nonpublic forum, then the university's action would have been judged on a reasonableness standard.

The court looked at four factors in determining whether the yearbook was a public forum: (1) university policy; (2) university practice; (3) the nature of the property at issue and its compatibility with expressive activity; and (4) the context in which the property is found.

"Evaluating these factors [. . .] we find clear evidence of KSU's intent to make the yearbook a limited public forum," the Court said. The university-written publications policy and the structure it created to oversee the yearbook gave editorial control to the student editors.

The court also noted that the record was clear as to actual practice: "Student editors, not KSU officials, not the student publications adviser and not the Student Publications Board, determined the content of KSU's student yearbook."

As for the nature of the property, the Court said the yearbook by its very nature exists for the purposes of expressive activity. "There can be no serious argument [about the fact] that [in its most basic form] the yearbook serves as a forum in which student editors present pictures, captions and other written material and that these materials constitute expression for purposes of the First Amendment," the opinion stated.

"As a creative publication, the yearbook is easily distinguished from other government fora whose natures are not so compatible with free expression. It is difficult to conceive of a forum whose nature is more compatible with expression."

As noted earlier, the Court thought the college connection was important: "The fact that the forum at issue arises in the university context mitigates in favor of finding that the yearbook is a limited public forum."

## Unreasonable College Student Censorship

Once the Court determined that the yearbook was a public forum, it then applied the "compelling interest" standard to the conduct of the university in its dealings with the yearbook. It found the university's action in confiscating the yearbooks a violation of the First Amendment, and "the university has no constitutionally valid reason to withhold distribution."

The Court used strong language in condemning the university: "Confiscation ranks with forced government speech as amongst the purest form of content alteration. [. . .] We will not sanction a reading of the First Amendment that permits government officials to censor expression in a limited public forum in order to coerce speech that pleases the government."

But what's even more remarkable about the decision is the court's determination that KSU's actions would violate the First Amendment even if the yearbook were found to be a nonpublic forum.

"These facts show without doubt," said the Court, "that the university's confiscation of the yearbooks was anything but reasonable; rather, it was a rash, arbitrary act, wholly out of proportion to the situation it was allegedly intended to address."

Then, noting that even in a nonpublic forum government cannot engage in viewpoint discrimination, the Court said the suppression of the yearbook "smacks of viewpoint discrimination as well."

It is unclear whether other courts will apply a public forum analysis in future cases involving public college media censorship. But such analysis seems appropriate when dealing with such government-owned property.

In fact, in footnote six of the decision, the Court writes: "Our decision to apply the forum doctrine to the student yearbook at issue in this case has no bearing on the question of whether and the extent to which a public university may alter the content of a student newspaper. Likewise, we note that a college yearbook with features akin to a university student newspaper might be analyzed under a framework other than the forum framework."

If other federal circuits adopt the reasoning of this case, public college officials will find it virtually impossible to control the content of student media without running afoul of the First Amendment.

Most public college newspapers and yearbooks, like the yearbook at Kentucky State, would be designated public forums. Thus, content control by administrators would have to meet a "compelling interest" standard. In the vast majority of censorship controversies, such a standard could not be met.

A college could try to establish policies and engage in practices regarding its student media that negate a finding of a public forum. But even if it did and a reasonableness standard was applied to censorship actions, *Kincaid* still would find those actions unconstitutional.

College student media usually run afoul of college officials because content is embarrassing, it upsets a segment of the community or the officials disagree with the point of view expressed. Under the analysis of *Kincaid*, such censorship actions would not be reasonable.

> *"School officials in this case did not violate the First Amendment by confiscating the pro-drug banner and suspending the student responsible for it."*

# Student Speech Advocating Drug Use Is Not Protected Expression

## The Supreme Court's Decision

### John Roberts

*In the following viewpoint Chief Justice John Roberts, writing for the majority of the Court, claims that the First Amendment does not protect student speech that advocates drug use at a school-sanctioned event. The Court contends that advocating drug use is different from expressing a political view about drug laws. The Court claims that the problem of drug use among young people, coupled with the legitimate interest schools have in curbing student drug use, makes restriction of student expression advocating drug use a reasonable goal. Thus, this decision further limits protected student expression—both at school or during school events—if that expression can be seen to collide with the school's goal of deterring drug use. Roberts is the US Supreme Court's chief justice, appointed by President George W. Bush in 2005.*

At a school-sanctioned and school-supervised event, a high school principal saw some of her students unfurl a large banner conveying a message she reasonably regarded as promoting illegal drug use. Consistent with established school policy prohibiting such messages at school events, the principal directed the students to take down the banner. One student—among those who had brought the banner to the event—refused to do so. The principal confiscated the banner and later suspended the student. The Ninth Circuit held that the principal's actions violated the First Amendment, and that the student could sue the principal for damages.

Our cases make clear that students do not "shed their constitutional rights to freedom of speech or expression at the schoolhouse gate" [*Tinker v. Des Moines Independent Community School Dist.* (1969)]. At the same time, we have held that "the constitutional rights of students in public school are not automatically coextensive with the rights of adults in other settings," [*Bethel School Dist. No. 403 v. Fraser* (1986)], and that the rights of students "must be 'applied in light of the special characteristics of the school environment'" [*Hazelwood School Dist. v. Kuhlmeier* (1988) (quoting *Tinker*)]. Consistent with these principles, we hold that schools may take steps to safeguard those entrusted to their care from speech that can reasonably be regarded as encouraging illegal drug use. We conclude that the school officials in this case did not violate the First Amendment by confiscating the pro-drug banner and suspending the student responsible for it.

## A Student Suspension for a Banner

On January 24, 2002, the Olympic Torch Relay passed through Juneau, Alaska, on its way to the winter games in Salt Lake City, Utah. The torchbearers were to proceed along a street in front of Juneau-Douglas High School (JDHS) while school was in session. Petitioner Deborah Morse, the school principal, decided to permit staff and students to participate in the Torch Relay as an approved social event or class trip. Students were allowed to leave class to observe the relay from either side of the street. Teachers and administrative officials monitored the students' actions.

Respondent Joseph Frederick, a JDHS senior, was late to school that day. When he arrived, he joined his friends (all but one of whom were JDHS students) across the street from the school to watch the event. Not all the students waited patiently. Some became rambunctious, throwing plastic cola bottles and snowballs and scuffling with their classmates. As the torchbearers and camera crews passed by, Frederick and his friends unfurled a 14-foot banner bearing the phrase: "BONG HiTS 4 JESUS." The large banner was easily readable by the students on the other side of the street.

Principal Morse immediately crossed the street and demanded that the banner be taken down. Everyone but Frederick complied. Morse confiscated the banner and told Frederick to report to her office, where she suspended him for 10 days. Morse later explained that she told Frederick to take the banner down because she thought it encouraged illegal drug use, in violation of established school policy. Juneau School Board Policy No. 5520 states: "The Board specifically prohibits any assembly or public expression that . . . advocates the use of substances that are illegal to minors. . . . " In addition, Juneau School Board Policy No. 5850 subjects "[p]upils who participate in approved social events and class trips" to the same student conduct rules that apply during the regular school program.

Frederick administratively appealed his suspension, but the Juneau School District Superintendent upheld it, limiting it to time served (8 days). In a memorandum setting forth his reasons, the superintendent determined that Frederick had displayed his banner "in the midst of his fellow students, during school hours, at a school-sanctioned activity." He further explained that Frederick "was not disciplined because the principal of the school 'disagreed' with his message, but because his speech appeared to advocate the use of illegal drugs."

The superintendent continued:

The common-sense understanding of the phrase "bong hits" is that it is a reference to a means of smoking marijuana. Given [Frederick's] inability or unwillingness to express any other credible meaning for the phrase, I can only agree with the principal and countless others who saw the banner as advocating the use of illegal drugs. [Frederick's] speech was not political. He was not advocating the legalization of marijuana or promoting a religious belief. He was displaying a fairly silly message promoting illegal drug usage in the midst of a school activity, for the benefit of television cameras covering the Torch Relay. [Frederick's] speech was potentially disruptive to the event and clearly disruptive of and inconsistent with the school's educational mission to educate students about the dangers of illegal drugs and to discourage their use.

Relying on our decision in *Fraser*, the superintendent concluded that the principal's actions were permissible because Frederick's banner was "speech or action that intrudes upon the work of the schools." The Juneau School District Board of Education upheld the suspension. . . .

## A School-Sanctioned Event

At the outset, we reject Frederick's argument that this is not a school speech case—as has every other authority to address the question. The event occurred during normal school hours. It was sanctioned by Principal Morse "as an approved social event or class trip," and the school district's rules expressly provide that pupils in "approved social events and class trips are subject to district rules for student conduct." Teachers and administrators were interspersed among the students and charged with supervising them. The high school band and cheerleaders performed. Frederick, standing among other JDHS students across the street from the school, directed his banner toward the school, making it plainly visible to most students. Under these circumstances,

we agree with the superintendent that Frederick cannot "stand in the midst of his fellow students, during school hours, at a school-sanctioned activity and claim he is not at school." There is some uncertainty at the outer boundaries as to when courts should apply school-speech precedents, but not on these facts.

The message on Frederick's banner is cryptic. It is no doubt offensive to some, perhaps amusing to others. To still others, it probably means nothing at all. Frederick himself claimed "that the words were just nonsense meant to attract television cameras." But Principal Morse thought the banner would be interpreted by those viewing it as promoting illegal drug use, and that interpretation is plainly a reasonable one.

As Morse later explained in a declaration, when she saw the sign, she thought that "the reference to a 'bong hit' would be widely understood by high school students and others as referring to smoking marijuana." She further believed that "display of the banner would be construed by students, District personnel, parents and others witnessing the display of the banner, as advocating or promoting illegal drug use"—in violation of school policy.

## A Message of Drug Advocacy

We agree with Morse. At least two interpretations of the words on the banner demonstrate that the sign advocated the use of illegal drugs. First, the phrase could be interpreted as an imperative: "[Take] bong hits . . ."—a message equivalent, as Morse explained in her declaration, to "smoke marijuana" or "use an illegal drug." Alternatively, the phrase could be viewed as celebrating drug use—"bong hits [are a good thing]," or "[we take] bong hits"—and we discern no meaningful distinction between celebrating illegal drug use in the midst of fellow students and outright advocacy or promotion.

The pro-drug interpretation of the banner gains further plausibility given the paucity of alternative meanings the banner might bear. The best Frederick can come up with is that the banner is "meaningless and funny." The dissent similarly refers to the sign's message as "curious," "ambiguous," "nonsense," "ridiculous," "obscure," "silly," "quixotic," and "stupid." Gibberish is surely a possible interpretation of the words on the banner, but it is not the only one, and dismissing the banner as meaningless ignores its undeniable reference to illegal drugs.

The dissent mentions Frederick's "credible and uncontradicted explanation for the message—he just wanted to get on television." But that is a description of Frederick's *motive* for displaying the banner; it is not an interpretation of what the banner says. The *way* Frederick was going to fulfill his ambition of appearing on television was by unfurling a pro-drug banner at a school event, in the presence of teachers and fellow students.

Elsewhere in its opinion, the dissent emphasizes the importance of political speech and the need to foster "national debate about a serious issue," as if to suggest that the banner is political speech. But not even Frederick argues that the banner conveys any sort of political or religious message. Contrary to the dissent's suggestion, this is plainly not a case about political debate over the criminalization of drug use or possession.

## The Issue of Political Student Expression

The question thus becomes whether a principal may, consistent with the First Amendment, restrict student speech at a school event, when that speech is reasonably viewed as promoting illegal drug use. We hold that she may.

In *Tinker*, this Court made clear that "First Amendment rights, applied in light of the special characteristics of the school environment, are available to teachers and students." *Tinker* involved a group of high school students who decided to wear black armbands to protest the Vietnam War. School officials learned of the plan and then adopted a policy prohibiting students from wearing armbands. When several students nonetheless wore armbands to school, they were suspended. The students sued, claiming that their First Amendment rights had been violated, and this Court agreed.

*Tinker* held that student expression may not be suppressed unless school officials reasonably conclude that it will "materially and substantially disrupt the work and discipline of the school." The essential facts of *Tinker* are quite stark, implicating concerns at the heart of the First Amendment. The students sought to engage in political speech, using the armbands to express their "disapproval of the Vietnam hostilities and their advocacy of a truce, to make their views known, and, by their example, to influence others to adopt them." Political speech, of course, is "at the core of what the First Amendment is designed to protect" [*Virginia v. Black* (2003)]. The only interest the Court discerned underlying the school's actions was the "mere desire to avoid the discomfort and unpleasantness that always accompany an unpopular viewpoint," or "an urgent wish to avoid the controversy which might result from the expression" [*Tinker*]. That interest was not enough to justify banning "a silent, passive expression of opinion, unaccompanied by any disorder or disturbance."

## The Limits of Student Expression

This Court's next student speech case was *Fraser*. Matthew Fraser was suspended for delivering a speech before a high school assembly in which he employed what this Court called "an elaborate, graphic, and explicit sexual metaphor." Analyzing the case under *Tinker*, the District Court and Court of Appeals found no disruption, and therefore no basis for disciplining Fraser. This Court reversed, holding that the "School District acted entirely within its permissible authority in imposing sanctions upon Fraser in response to his offensively lewd and indecent speech."

The mode of analysis employed in *Fraser* is not entirely clear. The Court was plainly attuned to the content of Fraser's speech,

*The US Supreme Court ruled that Deborah Morse (left) was justified in suspending a student for unfurling a sign that read "BONG HiTS 4 JESUS" during a school activity because the sign could be interpreted as encouraging illegal drug use.* © AP Images/Evan Vucci.

citing the "marked distinction between the political 'message' of the armbands in *Tinker* and the sexual content of [Fraser's] speech." But the Court also reasoned that school boards have the authority to determine "what manner of speech in the classroom or in school assembly is inappropriate."

We need not resolve this debate to decide this case. For present purposes, it is enough to distill from *Fraser* two basic principles. First, *Fraser's* holding demonstrates that "the constitutional rights of students in public school are not automatically coextensive with the rights of adults in other settings." Had Fraser delivered the same speech in a public forum outside the school context, it would have been protected. In school, however, Fraser's First Amendment rights were circumscribed "in light of the special characteristics of the school environment." Second, *Fraser* established that the mode of analysis set forth in *Tinker* is not absolute. Whatever approach *Fraser* employed, it certainly did not conduct the "substantial disruption" analysis prescribed by *Tinker*.

## Expression at School

Our most recent student speech case, *Kuhlmeier*, concerned "expressive activities that students, parents, and members of the public might reasonably perceive to bear the imprimatur of the school." Staff members of a high school newspaper sued their school when it chose not to publish two of their articles. The Court of Appeals analyzed the case under *Tinker*, ruling in favor of the students because it found no evidence of material disruption to classwork or school discipline. This Court reversed, holding that "educators do not offend the First Amendment by exercising editorial control over the style and content of student speech in school-sponsored expressive activities so long as their actions are reasonably related to legitimate pedagogical concerns."

*Kuhlmeier* does not control this case because no one would reasonably believe that Frederick's banner bore the school's imprimatur. The case is nevertheless instructive because it confirms both principles cited above. *Kuhlmeier* acknowledged that schools may regulate some speech "even though the government could not censor similar speech outside the school." And, like *Fraser*, it confirms that the rule of *Tinker* is not the only basis for restricting student speech.

Drawing on the principles applied in our student speech cases, we have held in the Fourth Amendment context that "while children assuredly do not 'shed their constitutional rights . . . at the schoolhouse gate,' . . . the nature of those rights is what is appropriate for children in school" [*Vernonia School Dist. 47J v. Acton* (1995) (quoting *Tinker*)]. In particular, "the school setting requires some easing of the restrictions to which searches by public authorities are ordinarily subject" [*New Jersey v. T.L.O.* (1985)].

## A Compelling Interest in Decreasing Drug Use

Even more to the point, these cases also recognize that deterring drug use by schoolchildren is an "important—indeed, perhaps compelling" interest [*Vernonia*]. Drug abuse can cause severe and permanent damage to the health and well-being of young people:

> School years are the time when the physical, psychological, and addictive effects of drugs are most severe. Maturing nervous systems are more critically impaired by intoxicants than mature ones are; childhood losses in learning are lifelong and profound; children grow chemically dependent more quickly than adults, and their record of recovery is depressingly poor. And of course the effects of a drug-infested school are visited not just upon the users, but upon the entire student body and faculty, as the educational process is disrupted.

Just five years ago, we wrote: "The drug abuse problem among our Nation's youth has hardly abated since *Vernonia* was decided in 1995. In fact, evidence suggests that it has only grown worse" [*Board of Education v. Earls* (2002)].

The problem remains serious today. About half of American 12th graders have used an illicit drug, as have more than a third of 10th graders and about one fifth of 8th graders. Nearly one in four 12th graders has used an illicit drug in the past month. Some 25% of high schoolers say that they have been offered, sold, or given an illegal drug on school property within the past year.

Congress has declared that part of a school's job is educating students about the dangers of illegal drug use. It has provided billions of dollars to support state and local drug-prevention programs, and required that schools receiving federal funds under the Safe and Drug-Free Schools and Communities Act of 1994 certify that their drug prevention programs "convey a clear and consistent message that . . . the illegal use of drugs [is] wrong and harmful."

Thousands of school boards throughout the country—including JDHS—have adopted policies aimed at effectuating this message. Those school boards knew that peer pressure is perhaps "the single most important factor leading schoolchildren to take drugs," and that students are more likely to use drugs when the norms in school appear to tolerate such behavior [*Earls* (Breyer, J., concurring)]. Student speech celebrating illegal drug use at a school event, in the presence of school administrators and teachers, thus poses a particular challenge for school officials working to protect those entrusted to their care from the dangers of drug abuse.

## A Reasonable Restriction of Student Expression

The "special characteristics of the school environment" [*Tinker*], and the governmental interest in stopping student drug abuse—reflected in the policies of Congress and myriad school boards, including JDHS—allow schools to restrict student expression that they reasonably regard as promoting illegal drug use. *Tinker* warned that schools may not prohibit student speech because of "undifferentiated fear or apprehension of disturbance" or "a mere desire to avoid the discomfort and unpleasantness that always accompany an unpopular viewpoint." The danger here is far more serious and palpable. The particular concern to prevent student drug abuse at issue here, embodied in established school policy, extends well beyond an abstract desire to avoid controversy. . . .

School principals have a difficult job, and a vitally important one. When Frederick suddenly and unexpectedly unfurled his banner, Morse had to decide to act—or not act—on the spot. It was reasonable for her to conclude that the banner promoted illegal drug use—in violation of established school policy—and that failing to act would send a powerful message to the students in her charge, including Frederick, about how serious the school was about the dangers of illegal drug use. The First Amendment does not require schools to tolerate at school events student expression that contributes to those dangers.

> "Overall, the plaintiffs' perceptions reflect
> an appreciation for the experience that
> outweighs winning or losing."

# Student Plaintiffs in *Tinker*, *Hazelwood*, and *Morse* Recall Their Fights for Free Expression

## Personal Narrative

### Perry A. Zirkel

*In the following viewpoint Perry A. Zirkel interviews student plaintiffs from three student speech cases that went to the US Supreme Court:* Tinker v. Des Moines Independent Community School District *(1969),* Hazelwood School District v. Kuhlmeier *(1988), and* Morse v. Frederick *(2007). Mary Beth Tinker looks back on the victory in* Tinker *and says it encouraged her to speak up. Cathy Kuhlmeier says that her loss in* Hazelwood *steered her away from journalism. Joseph Frederick contends that the Court's decision in* Morse *was a mistake, and he claims that his speech should have been protected. Zirkel explores the way all three fought for their freedoms. Zirkel is professor of education and law at Lehigh University in Bethlehem, Pennsylvania.*

In the June 2009 issue of [*Phi Delta*] *Kappan*, my nominations for the all-stars in the constellation of the Supreme Court school law decisions included three First Amendment student speech cases—the landmark student rights victory in *Tinker v. Des Moines Independent Community School District* (1969) and the subsequent student losses in *Hazelwood School District v. Kuhlmeier* (1988) and *Morse v. Frederick* (2007).

To synopsize the cases. . . .

- The *Tinker* Court held that public school officials may not prohibit student expression unless it materially and substantially disrupts the work and discipline of the school.
- In contrast, the *Hazelwood* Court ruled that, for prohibiting school-sponsored student expression, school officials need only justification that is reasonably related to legitimate pedagogical concerns.
- Continuing this less protective trend, the *Morse* Court ruled that this relaxed, reasonableness standard also applied to nonschool-sponsored student speech the principal perceived as prodrug.

The literature concerning these Supreme Court decisions is extensive. But, since little has been written about the plaintiffs' perspectives on their cases, we decided to track down a named plaintiff in each of these three cases to learn what happened to them after the court cases ended.

Here is an abbreviated look at our questions and their excerpted responses.

## The Student Plaintiff in *Tinker*

*Mary Beth Tinker*
*Age then (1965)—13*

*What were your reactions during the lower court decisions in this case?*

"I thought kids didn't have much right to express themselves in schools. We were up against powerful people like the school board, and so [I thought] we would . . . lose . . . ."

*What was the immediate reaction of the local community?*

"In Des Moines . . . there was a mixed reaction. We got postcards encouraging us . . . people threw red paint at our house . . . this woman [threatened] to kill me. [But] we always felt [it wasn't much] compared to what the kids [during the civil rights movement went] through. . . ."

*What were the immediate perceptions and feelings of your family?*

"[At first] my dad especially didn't really want us to wear the armbands because there had been a ruling against it. [However,] once we did, they understood . . . because they had raised us to speak up for our beliefs. . . . "

*What impact did the case have on you personally?*

"It encouraged me . . . not only to advocate for [children and teenagers] but to encourage them to speak up for themselves, which is even more important. It really encouraged me to be an active citizen in democracy . . . ."

*What are you doing now, and what impact did the case have on your life choices, including your selection of a college and a career?*

"[At first I didn't want a career that could be controversial so] I became a piano technician [and did] the things I believe in on the side. Then I became a nurse [which] can become . . . controversial [e.g., healthcare issues]. It's worked out all right anyway."

*Would you have done things differently in terms of the actions leading up to the suit if you had another chance?*

"We would have taken more photographs. . . . That's just . . . a joke but, in general, I think we would do things the same."

*How do you want to be remembered?*

"As a person who spoke up against injustice and . . . took action in helping to bring a better world, a world of peace and fairness."

## The Student Plaintiff in *Hazelwood*
*Cathy Kuhlmeier*
*Age then (1983)—est. 17*

*What were your reactions during the lower court decisions in this case?*

"We were very upset that they initially ruled against us because we felt we had a strong case. . . . [We] were ecstatic when the appellate court ruled for us. We remained hopeful and determined."

*What was the immediate reaction of the local community?*

"It was very mixed. Some thought I was a terrible kid because I stood up against the school, and others thought it was great that someone (especially a student) would challenge authority in efforts to get adults to realize their actions are not always correct."

*What were the immediate perceptions and feelings of your family?*

"My mother has always perceived me as an intelligent, independent person who is not afraid to speak up about anything. She has been very proud of me and always supportive."

*What impact did the case have on you personally?*

"I think it has made me a much stronger and determined individual and definitely a fighter. I will not back down [on] issues (I don't mean like physical fighting), but I stand up and use my voice. . . . "

*What are you doing now, and what impact did the case have on your life choices, including your selection of a college and a career?*

"I work in the corporate offices of [a large company] in the risk-management department and serve as the department [head]. . . . The entire matter had left such a sour taste in my mouth that I did not want to do anything related to journalism, writing, or anything close to it."

*Would you have done things differently in terms of the actions leading up to the suit if you had another chance?*

"Knowing what I know now, I would have done more research on [our] attorney's background and knowledge. . . . "

*How do you want to be remembered?*

"First and foremost as a good mother and wife. . . . Also, as a caring, considerate person, one who was not afraid to speak my mind and help others. . . . "

## The Student Plaintiff in *Morse*
*Joseph Frederick*
*Age then (2002)—18*

*What were your reactions during the lower court decisions in this case?*

"I did not want to take my case to court. Prior to any court filings, I proposed [having an open debate forum between the ACLU [American Civil Liberties Union] and school board attorneys, but the school board rejected it]."

*What was the immediate reaction of the local community?*

"I had embarrassed the high school, so rather than follow their own policies regarding trespass, the high school informed the Juneau police I was a drug dealer with lots of cash and drugs in my car and insisted I be arrested for trespass. . . . "

*What were the immediate perceptions and feelings of your family?*

"My father made me take drug screen tests for four straight months—all were negative—and the only apology I ever received came from my father, who said he was sorry for doubting me but wanted to make absolutely certain I was not into drugs."

*What impact did the case have on you personally?*

"I have since found that the constitutional violations of student rights occur far too frequently. . . . In the words of Albert Camus, 'I would rather die on my feet than live my life on my knees in submission to an unjust authority.'"

*What are you doing now, and what impact did the case have on your life choices, including your selection of a college and a career?*

"Taught English in China and am still in China studying at [the] university."

*Would you have done things differently in terms of the actions leading up to the suit if you had another chance?*

"[No.] I did nothing wrong. I [unfurled the banner] off school property and am in vehement disagreement with the Supreme Court decision. . . . "

*How do you want to be remembered?*

"As a modern day Henry David Thoreau who utilized nonviolent dissent to stand up to an authoritarian and abusive school system . . . ."

Overall, the plaintiffs' perceptions reflect an appreciation for the experience that outweighs winning or losing. Despite experiencing the legal system at different times and with different circumstances, they share a common priority on the first of the American individual freedoms. In addition to various intervening variables, including gender, personality, and backgrounds, age seems to be a significant factor in insights and memories of these three freedom fighters. For the rest of us, it helps to put faces on the names of these important cases.

| "The Free Speech Clause permits public schools to restrict student speech that intrudes upon the rights of other students."

# Schools May Restrict Student Speech That Attacks Other Students

## The Circuit Court's Decision

### Stephen Roy Reinhardt

*In the following viewpoint Judge Stephen Roy Reinhardt, writing for the majority of the United States Court of Appeals for the Ninth Circuit, argued that schools may limit student expression that violates the rights of other students. Supporting a school's decision to disallow a student from wearing a T-shirt with an antihomosexual message, the court gave the green light for schools restricting speech that could be harmful to other students. In particular, the court noted that speech that attacks members of minority groups, such as homosexuals, blacks, and Jews, was likely to cause harm to other students and could rightfully be restricted. On appeal, the case was vacated by the US Supreme Court, sending it back to the lower court where ultimately it was dismissed because the plaintiff had gradu-*

Stephen Roy Reinhardt, Majority opinion, *Harper v. Poway Unified School District*, US Circuit Court of Appeals for the Ninth Circuit, April 20, 2006. Copyright © 2006 US Courts for the Ninth District.

ated. Thus, the guidance for other courts remains unclear on this issue and will likely be the subject of further court cases. Reinhardt is a circuit judge on the US Court of Appeals for the Ninth Circuit. He was appointed in 1980 by President Jimmy Carter.

Poway High School ("the School") has had a history of conflict among its students over issues of sexual orientation. In 2003, the School permitted a student group called the Gay-Straight Alliance to hold a "Day of Silence" at the School which, in the words of an Assistant Principal, is intended to "teach tolerance of others, particularly those of a different sexual orientation." During the days surrounding the 2003 "Day of Silence," a series of incidents and altercations occurred on the school campus as a result of anti-homosexual comments that were made by students. One such confrontation required the Principal to separate students physically. According to David LeMaster, a teacher at Poway, several students were suspended as a result of these conflicts. Moreover, a week or so after the [2003] "Day of Silence," a group of heterosexual students informally organized a "Straight-Pride Day," during which they wore T-shirts which displayed derogatory remarks about homosexuals. According to Assistant Principal Lynell Antrim, some students were asked to remove the shirts and did so, while others "had an altercation and were suspended for their actions."

## Student Expression on a T-shirt

Because of these conflicts in 2003, when the Gay-Straight Alliance sought to hold another "Day of Silence" in 2004, the School required the organization to consult with the Principal to "problem solve" and find ways to reduce tensions and potential altercations. On April 21, 2004, the date of the 2004 "Day of Silence," appellant Tyler Chase Harper wore a T-shirt to school on which "I WILL NOT ACCEPT WHAT GOD HAS CONDEMNED," was handwritten on the front and "HOMOSEXUALITY IS SHAMEFUL 'Romans 1:27'" was handwritten on the back. There is no evidence in the record that any school staff saw Harper's T-shirt on that day.

The next day, April 22, 2004, Harper wore the same T-shirt to school, except that the front of the shirt read "BE ASHAMED, OUR SCHOOL EMBRACED WHAT GOD HAS CONDEMNED," while the back retained the same message as before, "HOMOSEXUALITY IS SHAMEFUL 'Romans 1:27.'" LeMaster, Harper's second-period teacher, noticed Harper's shirt and observed "several students off-task talking about" the shirt. LeMaster, recalling the altercations that erupted as a result of "anti-homosexual speech" during the previous year's "Day of Silence," explained to Harper that he believed that the shirt was "inflammatory," that it violated the School's dress code, and that it "created a negative and hostile working environment for others." When Harper refused to remove his shirt and asked to speak to an administrator, LeMaster gave him a dress code violation card to take to the front office.

When Harper arrived at the front office, he met Assistant Principal Antrim. She told Harper that the "Day of Silence" was "not about the school promoting homosexuality but rather it was a student activity trying to raise other students' awareness regarding tolerance in their judgement [sic] of others." Antrim believed that Harper's shirt "was inflammatory under the circumstances and could cause disruption in the educational setting." Like LeMaster, she also recalled the altercations that had arisen as a result of anti-homosexual speech one year prior. According to her affidavit, she "discussed [with Harper] ways that he and students of his faith could bring a positive light onto this issue without the condemnation that he displayed on his shirt." Harper was informed that if he removed the shirt he could return to class.

## The School's Response

When Harper again refused to remove his shirt, the Principal, Scott Fisher, spoke with him, explaining his concern that the shirt was "inflammatory" and that it was the School's "intent to avoid physical conflict on campus." Fisher also explained to Harper that it was not healthy for students to be addressed in such a derogatory manner. According to Fisher, Harper informed him that he had already been "confronted by a group of students on campus" and was "involved in a tense verbal conversation" earlier that morning. The Principal eventually decided that Harper could not wear his shirt on campus, a decision that, he asserts, was influenced by "the fact that during the previous year, there was tension on campus surrounding the Day of Silence between certain gay and straight students." Fisher proposed some alternatives to wearing the shirt, all of which Harper turned down. Harper asked two times to be suspended. Fisher "told him that [he] did not want him suspended from school, nor did [he] want him to have something in his disciplinary record because of a stance he felt strongly about." Instead, Fisher told Harper that he would be required to remain in the front office for the remainder of the school day.

Harper spent the rest of the day in the school conference room doing his homework. At some point during that day, Deputy Sheriff Norman Hubbert, who served as the school resource officer for Poway High, came in to speak with Harper. The complaint alleges that Hubbert "came to interrogate" Harper to "determine if he was a dangerous student." Hubbert, however, asserts in his affidavit that he and Harper had a "casual conversation concerning the content of the shirt . . . the Bible and [the] scripture reference on the shirt," and that the conversation was conducted "simpl[y out of] curiosity . . . to understand the situation."

Toward the end of the school day, Assistant Principal Ed Giles spoke with Harper. Giles had discovered earlier in the day that Harper attended the same church that he had previously attended, and that he "knew [Harper's] father personally and had attended Biblical studies that [Harper's] father led on Tuesday nights." According to Giles, he went to speak with Harper "out of respect to [Harper] and his family" and "to make sure he was alright." Giles told Harper that he understood "where he was coming from" but wished that he could "express himself in a more positive way." Giles also said that he shared the same Christian faith as Harper, but that as a school employee, he had to watch how he expressed his beliefs and that when he came to work, he had to "leave his faith in [the] car." Giles then asked Harper to "consider other alternatives that would be more positive and non-confrontational," including sponsoring activities through the campus Bible Club.

After his conversation with Giles, Harper remained in the office for the last period of the day, after which he was instructed to proceed directly off campus. Harper was not suspended, no disciplinary record was placed in his file, and he received full attendance credit for the day....

## Student Speech in Public School

Public schools are places where impressionable young persons spend much of their time while growing up. They do so in order to receive what society hopes will be a fair and full education—an education without which they will almost certainly fail in later life, likely sooner rather than later. The public school, with its free education, is the key to our democracy. Almost all young Americans attend public schools. During the time they do—from first grade through twelfth—students are discovering what and who they are. Often, they are insecure. Generally, they are vulnerable to cruel, inhuman, and prejudiced treatment by others.

The courts have construed the First Amendment as applied to public schools in a manner that attempts to strike a balance between the free speech rights of students and the special need to maintain a safe, secure, and effective learning environment. This court has expressly recognized the need for such balance: "States have a compelling interest in their educational system, and a balance must be met between the First Amendment rights of students and preservation of the educational process."

[*LaVine v. Blaine Sch. Dist.* (9th Cir. 2001)]. Although public school students do not "shed their constitutional rights to freedom of speech or expression at the schoolhouse gate" [*Tinker v.*

## Different Judicial Approaches to *Harper*

When a panel majority of the Ninth Circuit Court of Appeals ruled that a derogatory T-shirt worn by Tyler Harper intruded upon the rights of homosexual students, it justified its holding by emphasizing the need for minority students to receive special protection in the school environment. This holding produced a scathing dissent from one of the judges on the panel, who accused the majority of stretching facts of the case to fit the holding that it wished to endorse. To possibly achieve a greater consensus and more clarity to its holding, the Ninth Circuit might have chosen to apply another prong of the case that it chose for its analysis, *Tinker v. Des Moines Independent School District* [1969], and chosen to follow precedent from another Circuit to support its reasoning that Harper's T-shirt might have forecast substantial disruption of the school environment. The court also might have chosen to follow the precedent of *Bethel School District No. 403 v. Frazer* [1986] to find that Harper's T-shirt was offensive to other students and interfered with the school's duty of inculcating proper values to students. Finally, the court might have chosen to follow *Hazelwood School District v. Kuhlmeier* [1988] to find that Poway High School did not open a public forum with the "Day of Silence," and thus had a legitimate, pedagogical reason to exercise editorial control over Harper's T-shirt. The court reached the right outcome in *Harper v. Poway Unified School District* [2006], but there may have been other, better ways to achieve that outcome.

*Mark A. Perlaky,* "Harper v. Poway Unified School District: *The Wrong Path to the Right Outcome?*" Northern Illinois University Law Review, *vol. 27, 2007.*

*Des Moines Independent Community School District* (1969)], the Supreme Court has declared that "the First Amendment rights of students in public schools are not automatically coextensive with the rights of adults in other settings, and must be applied in light of the special characteristics of the school environment" [*Hazelwood Sch. Dist. v. Kuhlmeier* (1988)]. Thus, while Harper's shirt embodies the very sort of political speech that would be afforded First Amendment protection outside of the public school setting, his rights in the case before us must be determined "in light of [those] special characteristics" [*Tinker*].

This court has identified "three distinct areas of student speech," each of which is governed by different Supreme Court precedent: (1) vulgar, lewd, obscene, and plainly offensive speech, which is governed by [*Bethel School District No. 403 v.*] *Fraser* [1986]; (2) school-sponsored speech, which is governed by *Hazelwood*; and (3) all other speech, which is governed by *Tinker*.

In *Tinker*, the Supreme Court confirmed a student's right to free speech in public schools. In balancing that right against the state interest in maintaining an ordered and effective public education system, however, the Court declared that a student's speech rights could be curtailed under two circumstances. First, a school may regulate student speech that would "impinge upon the rights of other students." Second, a school may prohibit student speech that would result in "substantial disruption of or material interference with school activities." Because, as we explain below, the School's prohibition of the wearing of the demeaning T-shirt is constitutionally permissible under the first of the *Tinker* prongs, we conclude that the district court did not abuse its discretion in finding that Harper failed to demonstrate a likelihood of success on the merits of his free speech claim.

## The Rights of Other Students

In *Tinker*, the Supreme Court held that public schools may restrict student speech which "intrudes upon . . . the rights of other students" or "colli[des] with the rights of other students to be secure and to be let alone." Harper argues that *Tinker's* reference to the "rights of other students" should be construed narrowly to involve only circumstances in which a student's right to be free from direct physical confrontation is infringed. Drawing on the Fifth Circuit's opinion in *Blackwell v. Issaquena County Bd. of Ed.* (5th Cir. 1966), which the Supreme Court cited in *Tinker*, Harper contends that because the speakers in *Blackwell* "accosted other students by pinning the buttons on them even though they did not ask for one," a student must be physically accosted in order to have his rights infringed.

Notwithstanding the facts of *Blackwell*, the law does not support Harper's argument. This court has explained that vulgar, lewd, obscene, indecent, and plainly offensive speech "by definition, may well 'impinge[] upon the rights of other students,'" even if the speaker does not directly accost individual students with his remarks [*Chandler v. McMinnville Sch. Dist.* (9th Cir. 1992) (quoting *Tinker*)]. So too may other speech capable of causing psychological injury. The Tenth Circuit has held that the "display of the Confederate flag might . . . interfere with the rights of other students to be secure and let alone," even though there was no indication that any student was physically accosted with the flag, aside from its general display [*West v. Derby Unified Sch. Dist.* (10th Cir. 2000)]. While "[t]he precise scope of *Tinker's* 'interference with the rights of others' language is unclear" [*Saxe v. State Coll. Area Sch. Dist.* (3rd Cir. 2001)], we unequivocally reject Harper's overly narrow reading of the phrase.

We conclude that Harper's wearing of his T-shirt "colli[des] with the rights of other students" in the most fundamental way [*Tinker*]. Public school students who may be injured by verbal assaults on the basis of a core identifying characteristic such as race, religion, or sexual orientation, have a right to be free from such attacks while on school campuses. As *Tinker* clearly states, students have the right to "be secure and to be let alone." Being secure involves not only freedom from physical assaults but from psychological attacks that cause young people to question their self-worth and their rightful place in society. The "right to be let alone" has been recognized by the Supreme Court, of course, as "'the most comprehensive of rights and the right most valued by civilized men'" [*Hill v. Colorado* (2000) (quoting *Olmstead v. United States* (1928) (Brandeis, J., dissenting))]. Indeed, the "recognizable privacy interest in avoiding unwanted communication" is perhaps most important "when persons are 'powerless to avoid' it" [*Hill* (quoting *Cohen v. California* (1971))]. Because minors are subject to mandatory attendance requirements, the Court has emphasized "the obvious concern on the part of parents, and school authorities acting *in loco parentis* [in the place of a parent], to protect children—especially in a captive audience" [*Fraser*]. Although name-calling is ordinarily protected outside the school context, "[s]tudents cannot hide behind the First Amendment to protect their 'right' to abuse and intimidate other students at school" [*Sypniewski v. Warren Hills Reg'l Bd. of Educ.* (3rd Cir. 2002)].

## Verbal Assaults on Members of Minority Groups

Speech that attacks high school students who are members of minority groups that have historically been oppressed, subjected to verbal and physical abuse, and made to feel inferior, serves to injure and intimidate them, as well as to damage their sense of security and interfere with their opportunity to learn. The demeaning of young gay and lesbian students in a school environment is detrimental not only to their psychological health and well-being, but also to their educational development. . . .

In short, it is well established that attacks on students on the basis of their sexual orientation are harmful not only to the students' health and welfare, but also to their educational performance and their ultimate potential for success in life.

Those who administer our public educational institutions need not tolerate verbal assaults that may destroy the self-esteem of our most vulnerable teenagers and interfere with their educational development. To the contrary, the School had a valid and lawful basis for restricting Harper's wearing of his T-shirt on the ground that his conduct was injurious to gay and lesbian students and interfered with their right to learn.

The dissent claims that we should not take notice of the fact that gay students are harmed by derogatory messages such as Harper's because there is no "evidence" that they are in fact injured by being shamed or humiliated by their peers. It is simply not a novel concept, however, that such attacks on young minority students can be harmful to their self-esteem and to their ability to learn. As long ago as in *Brown v. Board of Education* [1954], the Supreme Court recognized that "[a] sense of inferiority affects the motivation of a child to learn." If a school permitted its students to wear shirts reading, "Negroes: Go Back To Africa," no one would doubt that the message would be harmful to young black students. So, too, in the case of gay students, with regard to messages such as those written on Harper's T-shirt. . . .

The dissent takes comfort in the fact that there is a political disagreement regarding homosexuality in this country. We do not deny that there is, just as there was a longstanding political disagreement about racial equality that reached its peak in the [1950s] and about whether religious minorities should hold high office that lasted at least until after the 1960 presidential election, or whether blacks or Jews should be permitted to attend private universities and prep schools, work in various industries such as banks, brokerage houses, and Wall Street law firms, or stay at prominent resorts or hotels. Such disagreements may justify social or political debate, but they do not justify students in high schools or elementary schools assaulting their fellow students with demeaning statements: by calling gay students shameful, by labeling black students inferior or by wearing T-shirts saying that Jews are doomed to Hell. Perhaps our dissenting colleague believes that one can condemn homosexuality without condemning homosexuals. If so, he is wrong. To say that homosexuality is shameful is to say, necessarily, that gays and lesbians are shameful. There are numerous locations and opportunities available to those who wish to advance such an argument. It is not necessary to do so by directly condemning, to their faces, young students trying to obtain a fair and full education in our public schools. . . .

## The Importance of Political Expression

In his declaration in the district court, the school principal justified his actions on the basis that "any shirt which is worn on campus which speaks in a derogatory manner towards an individual or group of individuals is not healthy for young people. . . . " If, by this, the principal meant that all such shirts may be banned under *Tinker*, we do not agree. T-shirts proclaiming, "Young Republicans Suck," or "Young Democrats Suck," for example, may not be very civil but they would certainly not be sufficiently

*A high court determined that shirts addressing members of a historically oppressed minority group in a derogatory way are harmful to students' welfare and educational opportunity, and that such speech is not protected in a school context.* © Hector Mata/AFP/Getty Images.

damaging to the individual or the educational process to warrant a limitation on the wearer's First Amendment rights. Similarly, T-shirts that denigrate the President, his administration, or his policies, or otherwise invite political disagreement or debate, including debates over the war in Iraq, would not fall within the [jurisdiction of the "rights-of-others"] *Tinker* prong.

Although we hold that the School's restriction of Harper's right to carry messages on his T-shirt was permissible under *Tinker*, we reaffirm the importance of preserving student speech about controversial issues generally and protecting the bedrock principle that students "may not be confined to the expression of those sentiments that are officially approved" [*Tinker*]. It is essential that students have the opportunity to engage in full and open political expression, both in and out of the school environment. Engaging in controversial political speech, even when it is offensive to others, is an important right of all Americans and learning the value of such freedoms is an essential part of a public school education. Indeed, the inculcation of "the fundamental values necessary to the maintenance of a democratic political system" is "truly the 'work of the schools'" [*Fraser* (quoting *Tinker*)]. Limitations on student speech must be narrow, and applied with sensitivity and for reasons that are consistent with the fundamental First Amendment mandate. Accordingly, we limit our holding to instances of derogatory and injurious remarks directed at students' minority status such as race, religion, and sexual orientation. Moreover, our decision is based not only on the type and degree of injury the speech involved causes to impressionable young people, but on the locale in which it takes place. Thus, it is limited to conduct that occurs in public high schools (and in elementary schools). As young students acquire more strength and maturity, and specifically as they reach college age, they become adequately equipped emotionally and intellectually to deal with the type of verbal assaults that may be prohibited during their earlier years. Accordingly, we do not condone the use in public colleges or other public institutions of higher learning of restrictions similar to those permitted here.

Finally, we emphasize that the School's actions here were no more than necessary to prevent the intrusion on the rights of other students. Aside from prohibiting the wearing of the shirt, the School did not take the additional step of punishing the speaker: Harper was not suspended from school nor was the incident made a part of his disciplinary record.

Under the circumstances present here, we conclude that the School's actions did not extend beyond the scope of the restrictions permitted by *Tinker*. . . . The Free Speech Clause permits public schools to restrict student speech that intrudes upon the rights of other students. Injurious speech that may be so limited is not immune from regulation simply because it reflects the speaker's religious views.

> "T-shirts may intrude upon our lives in
> the public sphere, but they're also our
> most vivid reminder that free speech is
> woven into the fabric of our culture."

# Free Expression on Clothing Is an Important Right for High School Students

*Greg Beato*

*In the following viewpoint Greg Beato argues that free expression through the T-shirt medium ought to be celebrated. Beato contends that controversy over T-shirts with various messages in public places, including high schools, has gone too far. Rather than resorting to dress codes and punishment in response to unpopular or controversial opinions on T-shirts, Beato claims that society ought to be more tolerant of different viewpoints expressed on clothing. In particular, Beato claims that high school students should be allowed to express themselves through messages on T-shirts, which he claims are protected by the US Supreme Court's understanding of the First Amendment. Beato is a contributing editor at* Reason *magazine.*

Greg Beato, "I'm With Stupid: The Perennially Embattled Free Speech Zone Over Our Chests," Reason.com, April 2008. Copyright © 2008 Reason Foundation. All rights reserved. Reproduced by permission.

On April 29 [2008] a grassroots army of teenaged billboards, provocatively packaged in combed cotton agitprop, will be deployed across the land. Their goal? Raise consciousness, spark discussion, and, if all goes according to plan, get thrown out of class. The occasion is the sixth annual National Pro-Life T-Shirt Day.

"When school administrators harass students, tell them they can't wear the shirt, it raises awareness," says Erik Whittington, director of Rock for Life, the group that organizes the event. "The media gets ahold of it. The word gets out. The more people who hear the phrase on the shirt, the more we educate people."

## Expression Through T-Shirts

This year [2008], Whittington says his organization has big plans. To promote Pro-Life T-Shirt Day, they're creating a Rock for Life website where the young pronatalist participants can network with each other. It'll be like MySpace or Facebook, except that instead of connecting over a common interest in drunken snapshots and copyright infringement, the teens will bond via a shared passion for fetuses. Even with such Web 2.0 accessorizing, however, the key to the event's potency remains the all-powerful T-shirt. "It has abortion in big letters," says Whittington of this year's model. "Then we have three graphics side by side. The first two are images of small children in the womb at early stages. The third image is blank. Under those images, it reads, Growing. Growing. Gone."

Considering all the incendiary polemics that characterize both sides of the abortion divide, this rhetorical dinger is fairly benign. Yet some kind of escalatory alchemy occurs when free speech is wedded to casual wear; the mildly provocative becomes untenable, the sophomoric too obscene to bear. Compared to sexier media devices like, say, the iPhone, T-shirts are pretty clunky. Their storage capacity is limited. They're not Bluetooth-enabled. And yet they boast a sense of intimacy and authority few other content delivery systems can match. They come, after all, with a living, breathing byline attached. They're far more mobile than other forms of meat-space spam [real-world advertising], such as billboards and posters; they literally get in your face.

## The Controversy over T-Shirts

In January of this year, several visitors wearing T-shirts emblazoned with various impeach-Bush-and-Cheney messages claimed that security guards at the National Archives Building—the place where the original version of the First Amendment now resides—barred them from the premises. In 1991, in the wake of the Gulf War, the Kuwaiti government sentenced one man to 15 years in jail simply for wearing a Saddam Hussein T-shirt. Today in the United States, we're far more enlightened: Selling a T-shirt inscribed with the names of military personnel who died in Iraq will only get you a maximum sentence of one year in Louisiana and Oklahoma.

Are you against sodomy or breast cancer? In favor of "hot moms" or John Edwards? In 2007 each of these convictions got at least one high school student kicked out of class. In Wisconsin, Edgerton High School enforces a zero tolerance policy against [rock band] Insane Clown Posse T-shirts. In Aurora, Illinois, all it takes to earn a trip to the principal's office is a T-shirt with a large dollar sign on it.

How did endorsing capitalism or B-list presidential candidates become so controversial? In the 1980s and '90s, hoping to crack down on intracurricular violence and crime, a growing number of schools resorted to the sartorial communism of dress codes and uniforms. As President Bill Clinton put it in 1996, "If it means that teenagers will stop killing each other over designer jackets, then our public schools should be able to require their students to wear school uniforms." In the wake of the 1999 Columbine High School massacre, message T-shirts and any other style of dress that undermined the notion that high school students were the new maximum-security inmates fell under suspicion. In the wake of 9/11—Columbine for adults—this at-

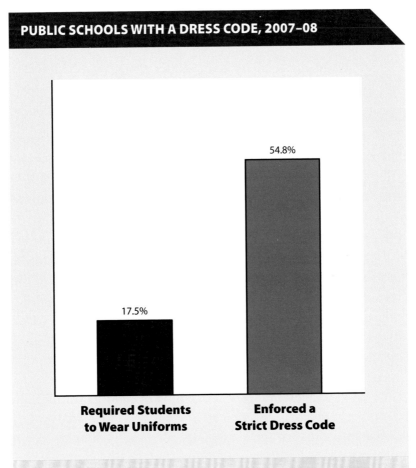

**PUBLIC SCHOOLS WITH A DRESS CODE, 2007–08**

54.8%

17.5%

**Required Students
to Wear Uniforms**

**Enforced a
Strict Dress Code**

Taken from: "Indicators of School Crime and Safety: 2010," National Center for Education Statistics, US Department of Education and Bureau of Justice Statistics, Office of Justice Programs, US Department of Justice, November 2010.

titude spilled over into our malls, airports, and presidential town hall meetings.

It's not just high school massacres and terrorist attacks that have left us so intolerant of our fellow citizens' chests. During the last decade, pretty much every major media innovation—Fox News, Google, Napster, iTunes, Digg—has involved filtering information more precisely, giving us more and more control over the data we ingest. But that uncompromising raw-foods zealot at the organic farmer's market whose shirt reads "Chewing is murder"? Or the perky fetus hugger who wants you to know that "Mean abortionists suck"? [Apple's] Steve Jobs hasn't figured out a way to delete them from your life yet.

## Embracing Free Expression

"If people don't want to listen to you, what makes you think they want to hear from your sweater?" the satirist Fran Lebowitz quipped in her 1978 essay collection *Metropolitan Life*, published when message T-shirts were enjoying their first wave of cultural ubiquity. What this sentiment doesn't acknowledge is that it's exactly because people don't want to listen to us that the drive-by evangelism of T-shirts is so enduring. Body-borne messages can't be muted, fast-forwarded, unsubscribed, banished to the "ignore" list, opted out of, or dumped in the recycle bin. Unlike telemarketers or Jehovah's Witnesses, they don't invade anyone's privacy. Their zero-decibel proselytizing is simultaneously low-key and obtrusive. . . .

Instead of avoiding such encounters with the dye-sublimated Other, we should embrace them as a kind of civic spinach: While we may not enjoy them, they're good for us. In *Tinker v. Des Moines*, the landmark 1969 case in which the U.S. Supreme Court determined that high school students have a First Amendment right to express political and social opinions in school settings, Justice Abe Fortas observed that "any word spoken, in class, in the lunchroom, or on the campus, that deviates from the views of another person may start an argument or cause a disturbance. But our Constitution says that we must take this risk; and our history says that it is this sort of hazardous freedom—this kind of openness—that is the basis of our national strength and of the independence and vigor of Americans who grow up and live in this relatively permissive, often disputatious society."

In the late 1990s era of no-logo vogue, cultural commentators fretted that the once-democratic medium of the T-shirt had been co-opted by corporations, and that T-shirt buyers were concerned only with raising the planet's Hilfiger consciousness and saving the FUBUs. "The slogans on contemporary T-shirts are increasingly meaningless," the novelist and columnist Russell Smith observed in *The Globe and Mail* in 2000. "Most of them are simply the brand name of the T-shirt itself."

## T-shirts in Public Schools

Now that our T-shirts are so blithely outspoken—and deliberately offensive—on every issue from Medicare to Britney Spears, it sometimes seems as if we'd like to ban our way back to a more sartorially decorous era. Ultimately, however, the T-shirt skirmishes that continuously erupt are oddly reassuring. Can the public schools be as out of control as they're often alleged to be if all it takes to get suspended from one is an "I ♥ My Wiener" shirt? Has our public sphere grown as hopelessly coarse as our loudest cultural scrub maids insist if a shirt featuring a faux

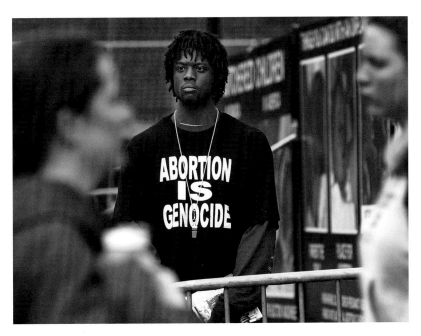

*T-shirts are contentious because they are highly visible and mobile without infringing on others' privacy.* © Mike Simons/Getty Images.

fishing theme and the phrase "Master Baiter" is enough to make Southwest Airlines ground you?

Shouldn't we take comfort in the fact that so many high school students are ready to fight for their right to champion the unborn, maternal hotties, and whatever else they can think of to test the limits of *Tinker v. Des Moines*? T-shirts may intrude upon our lives in the public sphere, but they're also our most vivid reminder that free speech is woven into the fabric of our culture.

| "Schools must remain cognizant of minors' rights to receive information protected by the First Amendment."

# Students Have a First Amendment Right of Access to Information

*Theresa Chmara*

*In the following viewpoint Theresa Chmara argues that the free-dom of expression guaranteed by the First Amendment protects not only the right to speak but also the right to receive information. Chmara claims that the US Supreme Court has decided that school boards may restrict speech or withhold information from minor students in certain circumstances, such as obscenity. Nonetheless, Chmara claims that school libraries need to ensure access by mi-nors to information except in limited cases. Cautioning schools to remain aware of minors' First Amendment rights, she claims that recent attempts to utilize filtering software for the Internet are dangerous because they allow in material that is obscene while also blocking information that is not obscene. Chmara is a Washington, D.C., lawyer and general counsel for the Freedom to*

*Read Foundation, a First Amendment legal defense organization affiliated with the American Library Association.*

The United States Supreme Court has long recognized that minors enjoy some degree of First Amendment protection. Students do not "shed their constitutional rights to freedom of speech or expression at the schoolhouse gate" [*Tinker v. Des Moines Independent Community School District* (1969)]. As one appellate court [*American Amusement Machine Association v. Kendrick* (2001)] posited so aptly, "[p]eople are unlikely to become well-functioning, independent-minded adults and responsible citizens if they are raised in an intellectual bubble." Recognizing that access to information is fundamentally necessary as a corollary to the right to speak, courts have held that minors' First Amendment rights include the right to receive information and extend beyond the classroom.

## School Restrictions on Speech and Access

For example, in *Board of Education v. Pico* (1982), the United States Supreme Court held that a school board's attempt to remove controversial titles such as *Slaughterhouse-Five* and *Soul on Ice* from the school library was unconstitutional. The Court stated that "the right to receive ideas is a necessary predicate to the recipient's meaningful exercise of his own rights of speech, press, and political freedom." The Court emphasized that "students too are beneficiaries of this principle." Through the years, the Supreme Court has recognized that "[s]peech . . . cannot be suppressed solely to protect the young from ideas or images that a legislative body thinks unsuitable for them" [*Erznoznik v. City of Jacksonville* (1975)]. Recognizing, however, that minors' exercise of First Amendment rights must be applied "in light of the special characteristics of the school environment" [*Pico*, quoting *Tinker*], the Court has acknowledged that the rights of minors are not equal to the rights of adults.

*The Children's Internet Protection Act of 2001 stipulates that to be eligble for some federal funds, schools must limit access to obscene materials, even if such blocking systems also limit access to constitutionally protected speech.* © AP Images/Kristen Wyatt.

The Court thus has permitted school boards to restrict speech or access to information for minors in two circumstances. First, school boards may restrict materials if they are motivated to do so because the materials are "educationally unsuitable" or "pervasively vulgar." School boards may not, however, censor materials if the removal is politically motivated and the restriction is based on disagreement with the ideas contained in the material.

Second, school boards may restrict materials that are obscene, harmful to minors, or child pornography. Whether material is obscene, harmful to minors, or child pornography generally is defined by state or local law. Definitions do vary from state to state. Moreover, a determination of whether material is obscene or harmful to minors is governed by community standards that may differ from state to state and town to town. Material deemed obscene or harmful to minors by a jury in one town might not necessarily be found to fit the definition of unprotected speech in another town. The jury must determine whether the material would be harmful to older minors, not all minors. For example, material cannot be deemed "harmful to minors" unless it fits the definition of obscenity for a seventeen-year-old. Material also cannot be deemed "harmful to minors" if it has any serious literary, artistic, political, or scientific value when evaluated as a whole.

Courts have also distinguished between the discretion accorded school boards in the realm of curriculum decisions as opposed to extra-curricular activities. School boards have broad discretion with respect to curriculum decisions. For example, in *Virgil v. School Board of Columbia County* (1989), the court of appeals affirmed a school board's decision to remove selected portions of *The Miller's Tale* and *Lysistrata* from a humanities course curriculum, stating that "[i]n matters pertaining to the curriculum, educators have been accorded greater control over expression than they may enjoy in other spheres of activity." In upholding the removal of material, the court emphasized that the disputed materials remained in the school library, which unlike a course curriculum, was a "repository for 'voluntary inquiry.'"

## The Internet at School

Internet access has posed the greatest challenge for educators and school libraries as they attempt to balance minors' First Amendment rights against concerns over the breadth of material that is posted and accessible online. There certainly are websites that would fit the definitions of obscenity, child pornography, and harmful to minors. There plainly is material on the Web that is educationally unsuitable and pervasively vulgar. At the same time, however, the Internet has become a powerful tool for educators and students in extending their reach for knowledge. The Web offers students a vast array of educational, cultural, and challenging learning experiences. Lawmakers, school boards, and school administrators must be cautious in limiting access to this powerful tool. Statutory restrictions on Internet access such as the Children's Internet Protection Act (CIPA) of 2001 and similar state provisions have limited access to material far beyond the categories the Supreme Court has held can be restricted. Filters restrict access to vast amounts of material that would be deemed "educationally suitable" for minors and could not be categorized as pervasively vulgar, obscene, harmful to minors, or child pornography.

CIPA provides that schools applying for certain funds for Internet access available in accordance with provisions of the Communications Act of 1996 (E-rate discounts) or the Elementary and Secondary Education Act of 1965 (ESEA) may not receive such funds unless the schools' administrators certify that they have in place a policy of Internet safety that includes the use of technology protection measures, such as filtering or blocking software, that protect against access to certain visual depictions available on the Web. Specifically, the school district seeking funds must certify that it has filtering or blocking software in place that will block access for minors to visual depictions that are obscene, child pornography, or harmful to minors. The school district must also certify that it has filtering or blocking software in place that will block access for adults to visual depictions that are obscene or child pornography. The technology protection measure must be placed on all computers, including those computers used by staff. The statute, codified at 20 U.S.C. § 9134(f)(3) and 47 U.S.C. § 254(h)(6)(D), provides that an administrator, supervisor, or other authorized person may disable the filtering software for adults, but only to enable access for "bona fide research or other lawful purposes." Federal law thus mandates use of a filter only if funds are accepted under these statutes. The CIPA statute does not mandate use of a particular filter. However, no existing filters can precisely block only visual depictions of child pornography, obscenity, and material harmful to minors. Thus, any filter used in a school necessarily will both over-block and under-block.

## Challenges to CIPA

CIPA was challenged in two lawsuits filed in the Eastern District of Pennsylvania. Both lawsuits alleged that application of CIPA in the context of the public library violated the First Amendment. On May 31, 2002, a three-judge panel held unanimously that the statute was unconstitutional. The court's holding was premised on the finding that "[b]ecause of the inherent limitations in filtering technology, public libraries can never comply with CIPA without blocking access to a substantial amount of speech that is both constitutionally protected and fails to meet even the filtering companies' own blocking criteria" [*American Library Association v. United States* (2002)]. The court also concluded that the disabling provision did not cure the unconstitutionality of the statute because requiring a patron to request access to constitutionally protected speech was stigmatizing and significantly burdened the patron's First Amendment rights.

In June 2003 the Supreme Court reversed the holding of the district court in a plurality opinion, with no majority opinion agreeing on all aspects of the reasoning in support of the reversal. The reversal was premised on the fact that six of the nine justices of the Supreme Court accepted the Solicitor General's assurance during oral argument that adults could ask that filtering be disabled without specifying any reason for the request. Thus, in the plurality opinion, Chief Justice [William] Rehnquist (joined by Justices [Sandra Day] O'Connor, [Antonin] Scalia, and [Clarence] Thomas) concluded that the statute was not unconstitutional because "[t]he Solicitor General confirmed that a 'librarian can, in response to a request from a patron, unblock the filtering mechanism altogether' . . ." and further explained that a patron would not "have to explain . . . why he was asking a site to be unblocked for the filtering to be disabled." The Court's plurality opinion contemplated that "[w]hen a patron encounters a blocked site, he need only ask a librarian to unblock it or (at least in the case of adults) disable the filter" [*United States v. American Library Association* (2003)]. The case left open the question of whether denying access to a particular person in a particular case would be unconstitutional. That challenge currently is pending in a case in the state of Washington.

A challenge to the application of filtering software to adults in public libraries is the issue in the case of *Bradburn v. North Central Regional Library District*, still pending [as of June 2011] in the federal court. In November 2006 the American Civil Liberties Union of Washington filed suit against the North Central Regional Library District on behalf of three library patrons and the Second Amendment Foundation. The suit alleges that the library violated the plaintiffs' First Amendment rights under both the federal and state constitutions by refusing to disable Internet filters at the request of adult patrons. The case was removed from the federal court to the Washington State Supreme Court for an initial determination of whether the library's refusal to disable filters (with no questions asked as to why the adult is requesting unfiltered access) violates the Washington State Constitution. Although it does not specifically address the issue of minors' rights, the Washington case is an important test of the reach of CIPA and the obligations imposed on libraries to disable filters. In May 2010 the Washington Supreme Court held that the Washington State Constitution does not prohibit filtering. The case will now return to the federal district court for a determination of whether the particular library filtering policy in place at North Central Regional Library violates the First Amendment of the United States Constitution.

## School Library Filters

To date, no challenge to the application of CIPA to schools, school libraries, or minors in any library setting has been made. The United States Supreme Court appeared to contemplate, however, that minors could ask for sites to be unblocked if they did not fit within the definitions of unprotected speech, i.e., sites that are obscene, child pornography, or material harmful to minors. Given that minors have explicit First Amendment rights, it would be prudent for schools—and particularly school libraries—to have a system in place to unblock sites that do not constitute obscenity, child pornography, or material harmful to minors.

Although there has been no challenge to date of a school library filtering system, schools must remain cognizant of minors' rights to receive information protected by the First Amendment. No filter can block accurately. Even with a filtering system in place, minors will be able to access material that is obscene, child pornography, or harmful to minors. Conversely, minors also will be blocked from accessing important educational and research materials when filters are used. Internet use policies should be drafted to balance these interests. Protecting minors' First Amendment rights and fulfilling the educational mission of promoting the greatest access to educational and research materials counsels for a system that allows school librarians and teachers to unblock sites with constitutionally protected material.

> "The First Amendment will protect many student postings, as long as they do not 'materially disrupt' school activities."

# Most Student Expression on the Internet Is Protected by the First Amendment

### Anita Ramasastry

*In the following viewpoint Anita Ramasastry argues that the First Amendment protects most student expression that takes place on the Internet, but there are exceptions. Ramasastry notes that illegal acts such as libel and threats are just as illegal on the Internet as elsewhere and are not subject to the First Amendment. For otherwise legal acts, Ramasastry cautions that sometimes school rules may limit a student's freedom of expression. Especially in cases of computer use taking place off campus, she says, public school officials are limited in their legal ability to censor or discipline. She notes, however, that there are exceptions when school officials can show that the expression online led to disruption at school. Ramasastry is the D. Wayne and Anne Gittinger Professor of Law and a director of the Law, Technology, and Arts Program at the University of Washington School of Law in Seattle, Washington.*

The past few years have seen the growth of popular social net-working websites for students: Three prominent examples are MySpace.com, Facebook.com, and Xanga.com. And within and outside such sites, student blogging, too, is wildly popular: About four million teens—19% of 12- to 17-year-olds who use the Internet—have created some sort of blog, according to a November 2005 Pew Internet & American Life Project study.

Unfortunately, however, such sites and blogs—despite all the good they've done for some students—have also created serious problems for other students, educators, and even law enforcement. No wonder, then, that many schools have blocked students from accessing such sites while on campus.

Students need to remember that the law applies in cyberspace too: Threats and harassment are just as illegal online as offline. Defamation or libel can occur on the Internet as well as in a printed newspaper. And when it comes to evidence of crime, the content of a personal website may be even more damning, in some cases, than a fingerprint.

But what about instances when student postings on networking sites aren't illegal, nor do they evidence or enable a crime—but, nevertheless, the postings upset school administrators or faculty?

In such cases, as I will explain, the First Amendment will protect many student postings, as long as they do not "materially disrupt" school activities—and as long as the students attend public, not private, schools.

## Social Networking Sites

I'll begin by giving readers the basics on MySpace.com and Facebook.com.

MySpace.com is currently [in 2006] the top social networking site on the web. It boasts up to 70 million registered users, of whom 25% may be teenagers.

Last July [2005], Rupert Murdoch's News Corp. bought MySpace for $580 million. Over the past year, traffic on MySpace has grown 318% . . . to 37.3 million visitors in February [2006].

MySpace says users must be at least 14. (The federal Children's Online Privacy Protection Act requires websites that target children under 13, to obtain "verifiable parental consent" before the kids can use the site; MySpace apparently didn't want to bother with the consent requirement.)

Free and ad-supported, MySpace allows users to post photos and music, and to stop by each other's sites to meet and mingle or hook up. Students can easily locate their classmates; MySpace

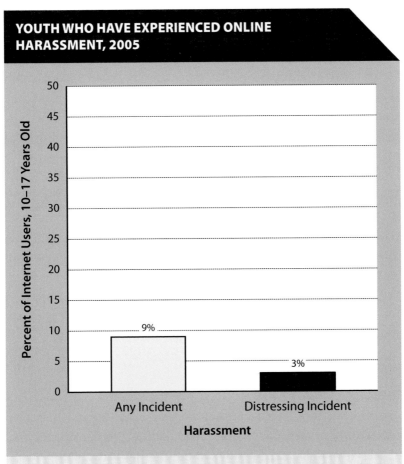

**YOUTH WHO HAVE EXPERIENCED ONLINE HARASSMENT, 2005**

Taken from: Janis Wolak, Kimberley Mitchell, and David Finkelhor, *Online Victimization of Youth: Five Years Later*, National Center for Missing and Exploited Children, 2006, p. 39.

maintains folders for various high schools and universities. Thus, MySpace can end up, in effect, hosting a virtual community that parallels a particular school or college—and often does.

But MySpace users need not belong to that community: If they so choose, they can customize their sites—blocking anyone but friends, for example. In addition, the site encourages users who feel they are being threatened by another member, to block that member and contact the police.

MySpace also reserves the right to terminate a user for engaging in threatening, lewd, or otherwise inappropriate behavior. And it will remove fake profiles by impersonators—a remedy that can be used by faculty, administrators or students who discover fake profiles claiming to be theirs.

Whereas MySpace.com is especially popular with teenagers, Facebook.com is especially popular with college students. Indeed, Facebook.com has claimed that it is used by 65% of undergrads at four-year colleges and universities. That amounts to more than 6.1 million students from more than 2,100 schools.

Last September [2005], Facebook expanded its reach to high-schoolers. At last count, a reported 900,000 had signed up.

Members can view full profiles of students from their own school. They can also search for other classmates by name, but if they locate them, they can see only the student's name, school and photo. To access a full profile, they must seek permission to be added to the student's list of "friends." Just as they can on MySpace.com, members also can impose further privacy limits—allowing access *only* to a chosen circle of friends.

## Cases in Which Postings Violate the Law

These sites—though a boon to students in many ways—have also raised their share of problems. And some of the problems may also involve torts, or violations of the criminal law.

In some instances, students engage in cyber-bullying— making critical remarks about other students or teachers. If these postings are factual, false, and damaging, they may count as defamation. The sites cannot be sued: Under a key provision of the Communications Decency Act, web intermediaries—those who merely allow others to post their own comments and photos—are not liable for defamation. But the authors can be.

Sometimes postings may be evidence of law-violation: In photos, underage subjects may be shown in sexually provocative poses, or shown smoking or drinking, or holding firearms. For instance, a 16-year-old boy in Jefferson, Colorado, was arrested after police—having seen pictures on his MySpace page in which he was holding handguns—found the weapons in his home. And in late April [2006], police reportedly intercepted a Columbine-style plot in Kansas on the basis of a threatening email posted on MySpace.com.

And sometimes postings may themselves violate the law—making criminal threats, or constituting harassment. In Costa Mesa, California, twenty students were suspended from TeWinkle Middle School for two days for participating in a MySpace group

*Some postings on social-networking sites can constitute evidence of a crime being committed, such as underage drinking.* © Scott Houston/Corbis.

where one student allegedly threatened to kill another and made anti-Semitic remarks.

Finally, sometimes postings can be an instrumentality of crime. Police have investigated allegations that teens were sexually assaulted by men they met on social networking sites. Indeed, the website Mycrimespace.com claims that various arrests of sexual predators are connected to users who have contacted their victims via MySpace.com

## Cases in Which Postings Violate School Rules

Even if postings don't violate the law—or evidence or enable its violation—they may still break school rules, or evidence that these rules have been broken. For example, a gay student was recently expelled from a Christian university after the university found photos of him in drag on his MySpace.com page. The university said the student had violated its code of conduct, because his behavior was not consistent with Biblical values.

Moreover, even if rules are not broken, the postings may still trigger administrators to want to take punitive action such as suspension, expulsion, or putting a note on the student's record that may harm his or her chances of college admission, or on the job market.

Do students facing such actions have a First Amendment defense? Private high school students may be out of luck: their schools are not "government" actors, and the First Amendment does not apply.

(Also out of luck are students who are foolish enough to publicly criticize schools before they attend them: The Admissions Dean at Reed College in Portland, Oregon, has noted that one [applicant] got rejected after disparaging Reed on the blogging site LiveJournal.com.)

In contrast, admitted students at public high schools, public colleges—and possibly private colleges that receive government money—may enjoy the First Amendment's protection for their online postings.

## Past Court Rulings

According to the U.S. Supreme Court, public school students don't "shed their constitutional right to freedom of speech or expression at the schoolhouse gate." Accordingly, in *Tinker v. Des Moines Independent Community School District* [1969], the Court said public high school students had a First Amendment right to wear black armbands to class to protest the Vietnam War.

Student free-speech rights can be limited when the speech "materially disrupts classwork or involves substantial disorder or invasion of the rights of others"—and the armband-wearing, the Court said in *Tinker*, didn't meet the test.

What kind of limitations have been upheld?

In *Bethel School District No. 403 v. Fraser* [1986], the Court ruled that a high school student whose student-government-nomination speech included "obscene, profane language or gestures" could constitutionally be suspended.

And in *Hazelwood Sch. Dist. v. Kuhlmeier* [1988], the Court okayed censorship of a school-sponsored newspaper that was "reasonably related to legitimate pedagogical concerns."

But the *Hazelwood* ruling was limited in important ways. It applied only to censorship of "school-sponsored publications, theatrical productions, and other expressive activities that students, parents, and members of the public might reasonably perceive to bear the imprimatur of the school"—and it did *not* apply to even school-sponsored publications that had been opened as "public forums for student expression." (Finally, it's clear the standard would not apply to college newspapers.)

Let's look at a few specific cases.

In 2000, a federal court in the Western District of Washington State held—in *Emmett v. Kent School District*—that public school officials could not punish student Nick Emmett for postings on a website, referred to as the "Unofficial Kentlake High

Home Page." Emmett and his friends—after being given the task of penning their own obituaries, in a creative writing class—had run afoul of school officials by posting a parody obituary for another classmate.

The court pointed out that at no time were school funds or computers involved with the website. Accordingly, the court held that "[a]lthough the intended audience was undoubtedly connected to Kentlake High School, the speech was entirely outside of the school's supervision or control."

Most courts to address such cases have agreed: When the publication originates off campus, a student has a First Amendment right to make even unpleasant, critical remarks.

## The Issue of Disruption

Occasionally, however, courts have applied *Tinker*'s "material disruption" standard even to off-campus speech.

For example, in 1998, in *Beussink v. Woodland School District*, a federal court in the Eastern District of Missouri inquired whether a public high school student's site using vulgar language to criticize his school and its faculty fulfilled *Tinker*'s standard. (As in the *Emmett* case, the site was created outside of the classroom, with the student's own computer and Internet connection; the court noted, however, that a classmate had viewed the site at school.) The court ultimately held that the site was First Amendment-protected because it was not materially disruptive.

Likewise, in 2002, in *J.S. ex rel H.S. v. Bethlehem Area School District*, the Supreme Court of Pennsylvania applied *Tinker* even though a website was not created at school, on the ground that the site "was aimed at a specific school and/or its personnel" and was "brought onto the school campus or accessed at school by its originator."

And there—unlike in the Missouri case—the court found a "material disruption" occurred: The site included an image in which a teacher's decapitated head dripped with blood and a request that visitors contribute $20 for a hit man. The site also showed an image of the same teacher's face transforming into Hitler's.

The "hit man" request came perilously close to a criminal threat or solicitation—a fact of which the court no doubt took notice. As noted above, when it comes to First Amendment protection here, we're talking about speech that isn't criminal: If a student publishes a physical threat toward another student, or a teacher or administrator, the Constitution won't protect that.

Criticism, though, is fair play. Just this month [May 2006], New Jersey's Oceanport School District . . . paid a $117,500 settlement to 17-year-old Ryan Dwyer after a district court ruled that it had violated his First Amendment rights by punishing him for a website blasting his middle school and some faculty members.

Mr. Dwyer wrote, among other things, "MAPLE PLACE IS THE WORST SCHOOL ON THE PLANET!" and "The Principal, Dr. Amato, is not your friend and is a dictator."

These messages—classic statements of opinion—weren't defamatory. They received full First Amendment protection.

> "The Internet . . . has fundamentally
> changed speech in ways that cry out for
> new guidance."

# Court Rulings Are Inconsistent in the Treatment of Student Expression Online

*Shannon P. Duffy*

*In the following viewpoint Shannon P. Duffy contends that a recent pair of decisions by the US Circuit Court of Appeals for the Third District illustrates that further clarity is needed on the issue of off-campus, online student speech. Duffy claims that the court's decisions appear to conflict with each other: One claims that online student expression is protected by the First Amendment precisely because the online expression took place outside of school. But the second claims that online student expression is not protected if it may cause a disruption at school, regardless of whether such expression took place on or off campus. Duffy recounts the reactions by lawyers and others to support the view that more clarity is needed on the free speech rights of students on the Internet. Duffy is US courthouse correspondent for the* Legal Intelligencer.

Lawyers were scratching their heads on Thursday [April 1, 2010] over a federal appellate court's seemingly conflicting rulings in a pair of closely watched student-speech cases that both involve high school students who were suspended for creating fake MySpace pages on their home computers to ridicule their principals.

## Two Conflicting Cases

Although the cases appeared at first glance to raise nearly identical legal questions about the limits on a school's power to discipline students for off-campus speech, the 3rd U.S. Circuit Court of Appeals sided with the student in *Layshock v. Hermitage School*

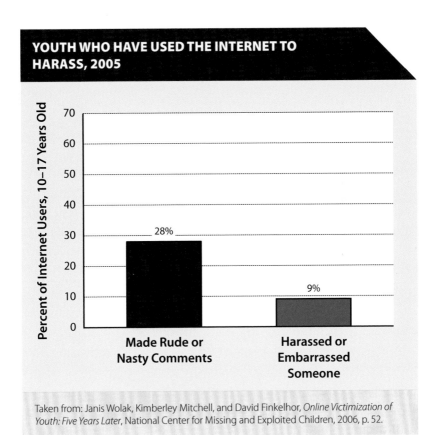

**YOUTH WHO HAVE USED THE INTERNET TO HARASS, 2005**

Taken from: Janis Wolak, Kimberley Mitchell, and David Finkelhor, *Online Victimization of Youth: Five Years Later*, National Center for Missing and Exploited Children, 2006, p. 52.

*District* [2010] and with the school in *J.S. v. Blue Mountain School District* [2010].

In *Layshock,* a unanimous three-judge panel declared that punishing students for off-campus speech violates their First Amendment rights. But the *Blue Mountain* panel split, voting 2–1 in holding that students may be punished for lewd speech on the Internet about school officials that has the potential to create a substantial disturbance at the school.

For lawyers watching the cases, it became clear during oral arguments in December 2008 and June 2009 that the two panels weren't likely to agree. Since federal appellate courts cannot issue conflicting opinions, court watchers predicted that the entire court might be forced to rehear both cases before an *en banc* [the entire] court.

Since *Layshock* was argued six months before *Blue Mountain*, some lawyers predicted that *Layshock* would be handed down first and its ruling would bind the panel in *Blue Mountain*.

But now the court has confounded the prognosticators by handing down a pair of decisions on the same day that reached opposite results.

## The Explanation for the Different Rulings

The court's explanation for the seeming conflict came in the *Blue Mountain* case, where the majority found there was no conflict at all, but instead that there were differences that made the two cases factually and legally distinguishable.

In *Layshock,* Judge Theodore A. McKee concluded that the student's suspension violated his First Amendment rights because the speech took place almost entirely off campus.

"It would be an unseemly and dangerous precedent to allow the state in the guise of school authorities to reach into a child's home and control his/her actions there to the same extent that they can control that child when he/she participates in school-sponsored activities," McKee wrote.

"Allowing the district to punish Justin [Layshock] for conduct he engaged in using his grandmother's computer while at his grandmother's house would create just such a precedent," McKee wrote in an opinion joined by judges Jane R. Roth and D. Brooks Smith.

But in *Blue Mountain*, Judge D. Michael Fisher concluded that school officials have the power to punish "student speech, whether on- or off-campus, that causes or threatens to cause a substantial disruption of or material interference with school or invades the rights of other members of the school community."

The Constitution, Fisher said, "allows school officials the ability to regulate student speech where, as here, it reaches beyond mere criticism to significantly undermine a school official's authority in challenging his fitness to hold his position by means of baseless, lewd, vulgar, and offensive language."

In dissent, Judge Michael A. Chagares said he believed that "neither the Supreme Court nor this court has ever al-

A pair of court cases came to opposite conclusions on the same day about whether schools have the authority to punish students for making inflammatory parody profiles on MySpace.
© Daniel Acker/Bloomberg via Getty Images.

lowed schools to punish students for off-campus speech that is not school-sponsored and that caused no substantial disruption at school."

Chagares complained that Fisher's decision "significantly broadens school districts' authority over student speech" and "vests school officials with dangerously overbroad censorship discretion."

Fisher, who was joined by visiting U.S. District Judge Paul S. Diamond of the Eastern District of Pennsylvania, said in a lengthy footnote that he was aware of McKee's decision in the *Layshock* case, but said "we find the two cases distinguishable."

In *Layshock*, Fisher said, the school district's lawyers never argued that there was "a nexus [link] between the student's speech and a substantial disruption of the school environment."

By contrast, Fisher said, the defense lawyers in *Blue Mountain* had argued at every step that the fake MySpace profile of the principal had caused actual disruptions at school and had the potential to cause more extensive disruptions if school officials had not responded quickly by punishing the students.

Fisher was impressed by the second prong of that argument, saying, "We are sufficiently persuaded that the profile presented a reasonable possibility of a future disruption, which was preempted only by [the principal's] expeditious investigation of the profile, which secured its quick removal, and his swift punishment of its creators."

Although the two cases at first appeared to represent a split of authority at the district court level, the 3rd Circuit's rulings effectively declare that there never was a split and, instead, that both of the lower court judges got it right.

In *Layshock*, Judge Terrence F. McVerry of the Western District of Pennsylvania found that school officials went too far when they suspended Justin Layshock for creating a fake profile of Hickory High School's principal, Eric Trosch, that said he was a "big steroid freak," a "big hard ass" and a "big whore" who smoked a "big blunt [marijuana cigarette]."

In *Blue Mountain*, Judge James M. Munley of the Middle District of Pennsylvania upheld a 10-day suspension of a student who posted a profile on MySpace in March 2007 that showed a photo of principal James McGonigle and described him as a pedophile and a sex addict whose interests included "being a tight ass," "f---ing in my office" and "hitting on students and their parents."

Munley concluded that the suspension was proper because school officials "can validly restrict speech that is vulgar and lewd and also it can restrict speech that promotes unlawful behavior."

By contrast, McVerry had concluded that since Layshock's prank took place off campus and none of the in-school events amounted to a true disruption of school activities, the school had no power to discipline him.

"The mere fact that the Internet may be accessed at school does not authorize school officials to become censors of the world wide web," McVerry wrote.

## The Need for Guidance

Both students were represented by the American Civil Liberties Union [ACLU] of Pennsylvania. Witold Walczak, the ACLU's legal director, said Thursday [February 4, 2010] that he found the two decisions "difficult to reconcile," and that he is considering whether to petition for a reargument of the *Blue Mountain* case before the full court.

The *Blue Mountain* decision, Walczak said, "gives school principals a seat at the dining room table in students' homes."

But the winning lawyer in the *Blue Mountain* case, Jonathan P. Riba of [the law firm] Sweet Stevens Katz & Williams in New Britain, [Pennsylvania], said he believes [Judge] Fisher properly recognized that a substantial disturbance was imminent and would have occurred if the principal had not acted quickly.

Attorney Anthony G. Sanchez, the losing defense lawyer in the *Layshock* case, said he believes the issue is ripe for review by the U.S. Supreme Court because the lower courts are struggling with a framework of student-speech jurisprudence that was laid down in the late 1960s and early 1970s.

The Internet, Sanchez said, has fundamentally changed speech in ways that cry out for new guidance because a student's off-campus speech can now be directed at the school community in ways that defy the temporal and geographic constraints that applied to speech of a few decades ago.

| "*Free speech rights of students have been curtailed.*"

# The Free Speech Rights of Students Are in Poor Shape Forty Years After *Tinker*

## Personal Narrative

### Stephen J. Wermiel

*In the following viewpoint Stephen J. Wermiel interviews Mary Beth Tinker for* Human Rights *magazine. Tinker was a thirteen-year-old junior high school student when she and other students decided to wear black armbands to school to express opposition to the Vietnam War, and were suspended by school officials for not taking them off when asked. The incident ultimately made its way to the US Supreme Court in* Tinker v. Des Moines Independent Community School District *(1969), the landmark student expression case that protected student rights to express political opinions. Tinker expresses her concern that the First Amendment rights of students are not as strong as they were following* Tinker, *and she urges young people to stand up for their rights. Wermiel is a fellow in law and government and associate director of the Summer Institute on Law and Government at American University Washington College of Law.*

**H**uman Rights: *What's the state of student free speech or student rights more broadly as we approach the fortieth anniversary of* Tinker?

**Mary Beth Tinker:** They are in about the same state as students' well-being overall, whether you're talking about health issues or educational quality or housing or access to clean air and water, which are not very good right now. And I'm speaking as a nurse who has worked primarily with young people.

For one thing, No Child Left Behind [a 2001 US education reform law] has not been helpful in teaching students about their rights or helping them to model democratic behavior. Curriculum directed toward standardized tests in math and science may "train" young people in certain skills, particularly test-taking skills, but are lacking in other areas. So, despite the valiant efforts of history and government teachers across the country, it is no wonder that we are seeing woefully poor indicators of students' knowledge of the First Amendment, for example.

Some states see rising test scores as success, but many of us who work with youths are skeptical. Critical thinking and creativity, which are so important to participatory democracy, have been sacrificed.

## Tinker After Forty Years
*How do you feel about the* Tinker *case itself after forty years?*

The *Tinker* ruling said that students had the right to free speech and other First Amendment rights unless their speech was "substantially disruptive" or intruded on the rights of others. So that was a foundation, because it's not a very high standard.

Since then, school districts have claimed that various activities are disruptive or intrude on the rights of others. The ruling leaves a lot of leeway for principals and school boards to attempt to censor students, and they often succeed.

Regardless, of course, I am happy that the [US Supreme Court under the guidance of Chief Justice Earl Warren] ruled in favor of students' rights. In a democracy, the people who are affected by decisions are supposed to be the ones who have the right to speak on their own behalf, and this should include young people. Today, I see so many examples of young people standing up for their own interests.

For example, students in Ohio recently developed the Ohio Youth Agenda, a collaboration of youths across the state advocating for improvement in schools, counseling, and education funding. Students in Maryland were featured in the *Washington Post* recently, picketing against a new polluting freeway near their school. Another Maryland girl, Sarah Boltuck, succeeded in getting state legislation passed that will allow seventeen-year-olds to register to vote if they will turn eighteen by the time of the election. Twenty thousand youths are affected.

At a school in Florida, students had to fight for the right to wear rainbow clothing and bring stickers to school. They eventually won. Alondra Jones, in California, challenged unfair funding of her school and changed the school funding system for the whole state. And these are just a few examples that come to mind.

*Over the forty years, though, other cases have eroded the protection that* Tinker *established. How do you feel about that?*

Free speech rights of students have been curtailed, certainly, but the erosion is not limited to students. And besides Court rulings like *Hazelwood* [*School District v. Kuhlmeier* (1988)], *Morse v. Frederick* [2007], or the recent *Jacobs* [*v. Clark County School District* (2008)] ruling in Nevada, students' free speech rights have been curtailed in other ways. For example, I understand that about 40 percent of high school newspapers have been eliminated in the last ten to fifteen years.

## Young People's Rights

*In the fortieth anniversary year of* Tinker *next year [2009], what are you celebrating?*

I will be celebrating the spirit of young people and their creative energy in standing up for their rights against all odds, and their humor and concern, which are so needed in this current period. And I will be celebrating a Supreme Court that stood with young people to affirm their rights.

*And what should students [throughout] the country think about or celebrate?*

I urge students to celebrate their right to speak out by becoming engaged in issues that are important to their lives, and to exercise their First Amendment rights and, indeed, all their rights.

*You've spent a lot of time speaking to student groups and accepting the mantle of a spokesperson for student rights since the* Tinker *decision. How do you see that role?*

My parents put their beliefs into action, and they were examples to me. My father was a Methodist minister, and my parents later became Quakers. They spent their lives working for peace and justice. Over the years, I also met others and heard their stories about standing up for what they believed in. These people motivated and inspired me. So that is how I see my role with young people, to educate and inspire them. Besides teaching them basic civics, I tell them real stories about people, mostly young people, from the past and present, who have changed the world.

For example, I may tell them about Barbara Johns, who was sixteen in 1951 when she called an assembly at her school in Virginia, rallying students for better conditions at their school. She later became a plaintiff in the *Brown* [*v. Board of Education* (1954)] case. Or I tell them about the childrens' march of 1904, where child factory workers presented Teddy Roosevelt with a demand to end their sweatshop conditions. These are just examples of the many true stories that I choose from.

And then I tell them about young people today who are involved in various issues, like the ones I talked about earlier, and others.

*Are you hopeful that young people will continue to stand up for their rights, that the courts and the country will become more appreciative of the rights of students again?*

Yes. I see examples all over the country of students who are standing up for what they believe in, whether it's for peace, clean air, clean water, uniform policies, religious freedom, animal rights, gay rights, Darfur [a controversial and war-torn region of Sudan]. There are so many issues students care about.

I hear about students who, themselves, wear different, meaningful symbols—whether it's T-shirts, armbands, or buttons. Some are involved in the political process, working for different candidates that support young people's issues. All of that's very heartening to me.

*How about the role of lawyers, courts, and law in defending student rights? What do you think has happened over the last decades?*

Young people cannot make progress without the support and alliance of adults, whether they're lawyers or nurses, like myself, or parents or community partners. And so young people need to have supporters in the community who advocate for them also and who help them to advocate for themselves. That's the way I see the role of lawyers.

Adults can use their skills and talents to promote young people and teenagers, who need these skills more than ever in today's world. Because the condition of young people today is not good. There are so many indicators, whether health indicators or indicators of educational success—for example, graduation rates, college rates. I just heard statistics that around 50 percent of Washington, D.C., high school students are graduating. I understand that only around 9 percent of those high school students are completing a four-year college degree program.

Economic opportunities for young people are not good, and so many children go without health insurance. The Children's Health Insurance Program has been under attack. So many areas exist where young people really need advocates, especially legal advocates, and people with all kinds of skills and talents.

## The Jurisdiction of Schools

*One of the great messages of* Tinker *was not to fear protest—that school officials should accept protest as an essential part of democracy and even of education. Have we lost sight of that message?*

Well, I think the political climate in the country discourages young people from speaking up. Protest is only one of those ways that students might want to speak up. And I think it's a big mistake in a democracy to discourage people from being involved in the democratic process, in whatever form that may take.

Throughout history a lot of our progress has been the result of people who were considered dissidents in their time; without encouraging a climate where free speech and dissidents' voices flourish, we won't benefit as much as we could as a society. And we'll be held back in our own development and in relationship to other societies that are encouraging these kinds of expressions.

*And what's your feeling about the Supreme Court's most recent decision—the Bong Hits [Morse] case?*

That case, where Joseph Frederick unfurled a banner saying "Bong Hits 4 Jesus," was about more than just the so-called frivolous message. When I spoke to him on the telephone before the case was argued at the Supreme Court, he told me how he came to put that on his banner. He said he did that because he had been studying the First Amendment and the Bill of Rights in school, and he wanted to test and see if he really had First Amendment rights or if it was just something that he had learned in school books.

So he wanted to put something on his banner, and if he had just said "Hooray for the Olympic torch" which was going by, he wouldn't have been able to test his rights. So he sure did pick something that would get the attention of the school and others: "Bong Hits 4 Jesus." But his real message was that students should have First Amendment rights. And that is a serious message.

I'm sorry to see that the Court has once again limited the rights of students, not only in terms of the content of the message, but also the school's jurisdiction seems to have been extended because Joseph was standing across the street from the school and there was some question about whether it was actually a school-sponsored event. That's a big issue being debated now in our country—how far does the school's jurisdiction reach? And this ruling seems to have extended that.

*Yes, we will have to watch and see how far the reach of school officials continues to expand. Thank you for taking the time to answer our questions, and thank you very much for your continued dedication to the rights of students.*

# Organizations to Contact

*The editors have compiled the following list of organizations concerned with the issues debated in this book. The descriptions are derived from materials provided by the organizations.*

### American Center for Law and Justice (ACLJ)
PO Box 90555, Washington, DC 20090-0555
(800) 296-4529
website: www.aclj.org

ACLJ is dedicated to protecting religious and constitutional freedoms. ACLJ has participated in numerous cases before the Supreme Court, Federal Court of Appeals, Federal District Courts, and various state courts regarding freedom of religion and freedom of speech. ACLJ has numerous memos and position papers available at its website, including "Protecting the Rights of Students."

### American Civil Liberties Union (ACLU)
125 Broad Street, 18th Floor, New York, NY 10004
(212) 549-2500
e-mail: infoaclu@aclu.org
website: www.aclu.org

The ACLU is a national organization that works to defend Americans' civil rights as guaranteed in the US Constitution. The ACLU works in courts, legislatures, and communities to defend First Amendment rights, the right to equal protection, the right to due process, and the right to privacy. The ACLU publishes the newsletter *Civil Liberties Alert*, as well as other publications, including "Letter to Principals and Educators About School Censorship."

## American Library Association (ALA)

50 E. Huron Street, Chicago IL 60611

(800) 545-2433 • fax (312) 440-9374

e-mail: ala@ala.org

website: www.ala.org

The ALA is the nation's primary professional organization for librarians. The ALA provides leadership for the development, promotion, and improvement of library services and librarianship in order to enhance learning and ensure access to information for all. The ALA publishes online the *Newsletter on Intellectual Freedom*, which reports attempts to remove materials from school and library shelves across the country.

## Center for Campus Free Speech

328 S. Jefferson Street, Suite 620, Chicago, IL 60661

(312) 544-4438

e-mail: center@campusspeech.org

website: www.campusspeech.org

The Center for Campus Free Speech was created by students, faculty, administrators, and others to protect and promote free speech on university campuses. The Center acts as a clearinghouse of information; provides specialized support to campuses; and connects concerned educators, administrators, lawyers, and students into a national network. The Center publishes a variety of reports and papers supporting free speech on campus including "Speech Codes and Other Restrictions on the Content of Speech."

## Center for Public Education

1680 Duke Street, Alexandria, VA 22314

(703) 838-6722 • fax (703) 548-5613

e-mail: centerforpubliced@nsba.org

website: www.centerforpubliceducation.org

The Center for Public Education is a resource center set up by the National School Boards Association (NSBA). The Center for Public Education works to provide information about public education and lead to more understanding about schools, more community-wide involvement, and better decision-making by school leaders on behalf of all students in their classrooms. Among the many publications available at the center's website is "Free Speech and Public Schools."

### Electronic Frontier Foundation (EFF)

54 Shotwell Street, San Francisco, CA 94110-1914
(415) 436-9333 • fax (415) 436-9993
e-mail: information@eff.org
website: www.eff.org

EFF works to promote the public interest in critical battles affecting digital rights, defending free speech, privacy, innovation, and consumer rights. EFF provides legal assistance in cases where it believes it can help shape the law. EFF publishes a newsletter and reports, including the report "Internet Blocking in Public Schools: A Study on Internet Access in Educational Institutions," available at its website.

### First Amendment Coalition

534 4th Street, Suite B, San Rafael, CA 94901
(415) 460-5060 • fax (415) 460-5155
website: www.firstamendmentcoalition.org

The First Amendment Coalition is a nonprofit public interest organization dedicated to advancing free speech, more open and accountable government, and public participation in civic affairs. The First Amendment Coalition offers free legal consultations, engages in litigation, offers educational programs, and participates in public advocacy. The Coalition's website includes First Amendment news and opinion, as well as a searchable database from the organization's legal hotline information service, Asked & Answered.

## Freedom Forum

555 Pennsylvania Avenue NW, Washington, DC 20001
(202) 292-6100
e-mail: news@freedomforum.org
website: www.freedomforum.org

The Freedom Forum is a nonpartisan foundation dedicated to free press, free speech, and free spirit for all people. The forum's First Amendment Center works to preserve and protect First Amendment freedoms through information and education. It publishes the annual report "State of the First Amendment," as well as numerous other publications, including "The Silencing of Student Voices."

## National Coalition Against Censorship (NCAC)

275 Seventh Avenue, Suite 1504, New York, NY 10001
(212) 807-6222 • fax (212) 807-6245
e-mail: ncac@ncac.org
website: www.ncac.org

NCAC is an alliance of fifty-two participating organizations dedicated to protecting free expression and access to information. It has many projects dedicated to educating the public and protecting free expression, including the Free Expression Policy Project, the Kids' Right to Read Project, The Knowledge Project: Censorship and Science, and the Youth Free Expression Network. Among its publications is "The First Amendment in Schools."

## National Youth Rights Association (NYRA)

1101 15th St. NW, Suite 200, Washington, DC, 20005
(202) 835-1739
website: www.youthrights.org

NYRA is a youth-led national nonprofit organization dedicated to fighting for the civil rights and liberties of young people. NYRA has more than 7,000 members representing all 50 states. It seeks to lower the voting age, lower the drinking age, repeal curfew laws, and protect student rights.

## People for the American Way (PFAW)

2000 M Street NW, Suite 400, Washington, DC 20036
(202) 467-4999
website: www.pfaw.org

PFAW is an organization that fights for progressive values: equal rights, freedom of speech, religious liberty, and equal justice under the law for every American. PFAW works to build and nurture communities of support for its values, and to equip those communities to promote progressive policies, elect progressive candidates, and hold public officials accountable. Among its publications on the topic of freedom of speech is the report "Back to School with the Religious Right."

## Rutherford Institute

PO Box 7482, Charlottesville, VA 22906-7482
(434) 978-3888 • fax (434) 978-1789
e-mail: staff@rutherford.org
website: www.rutherford.org

The Rutherford Institute is a civil liberties organization. It provides legal services in the defense of religious and civil liberties, and it aims to educate members of the public on important issues affecting their constitutional freedoms. The Rutherford Institute publishes commentary, articles, and books, including "The Future Looks Bleak for the First Amendment."

# For Further Reading

## Books

Floyd Abrams, *Speaking Freely: Trials of the First Amendment.* New York: Penguin Books, 2006.

Michael Kent Curtis, *Free Speech, "The People's Darling Privilege": Struggles for Freedom of Expression in American History.* Durham, NC: Duke University Press, 2000.

Kenneth Dautrich, David A. Yalof, and Mark Hugo Lopez, *The Future of the First Amendment: The Digital Media, Civic Education, and Free Expression Rights in America's High Schools.* Lanham, MD: Rowman & Littlefield, 2008.

Donald Alexander Downs, *Restoring Free Speech and Liberty on Campus.* New York: Cambridge University Press, 2005.

Anne Proffitt Dupre, *Speaking Up: The Unintended Costs of Free Speech in Public Schools.* Cambridge, MA: Harvard University Press, 2009.

Terry Eastland, *Freedom of Expression in the Supreme Court: The Defining Cases.* Lanham, MD: Rowman & Littlefield, 2000.

Stephen M. Feldman, *Free Expression and Democracy in America: A History.* Chicago: University of Chicago Press, 2008.

Christopher M. Finan, *From the Palmer Raids to the Patriot Act: A History of the Fight for Free Speech in America.* Boston, MA: Beacon Press, 2007.

Steven J. Heyman, *Free Speech and Human Dignity.* New Haven, CT: Yale University Press, 2008.

Nan Levinson, *Outspoken: Free Speech Stories*. Berkeley, CA: University of California Press, 2003.

Anthony Lewis, *Freedom for the Thought That We Hate: A Biography of the First Amendment*. New York: MJF Books, 2011.

Dawn C. Nunziato, *Virtual Freedom: Net Neutrality and Free Speech in the Internet Age*. Stanford, CA: Stanford Law Books, 2009.

Brad O'Leary, *Shut Up, America! The End of Free Speech*. Los Angeles: WND Books, 2009.

Erik Ringmar, *A Blogger's Manifesto: Free Speech and Censorship in the Age of the Internet*. New York: Anthem Press, 2007.

## Periodicals and Internet Sources

*Austin* (TX) *American-Statesman*, "Latest Definition of Free Speech Hinges on Wacky Teen Prank," March 20, 2007.

Paul J. Batista, "The Boundaries of First Amendment Speech for Public School Students," *JOPERD—The Journal of Physical Education, Recreation, and Dance*, March 2008.

Marsha Boutelle, "Uniforms: Are They a Good Fit?" *Education Digest*, February 2008.

Ethan Bronner, "The Clampdown on Teen Rights," *New York Times Upfront*, September 6, 1999.

Steven M. Brown and Howard J. Bultinck, "From Black Armbands to Bong Hits for Jesus: The 40th Anniversary of *Tinker*," *Phi Delta Kappan*, June 2009.

*Current Events, A Weekly Reader Publication,* "Curses! Should Students Be Fined for Using Foul Language?" January 20, 2006.

Alfred P. Doblin, "An Image of Hate Is Not Always Hate Speech," *Record* (Bergen County, NJ), September 24, 2007.

Maureen Downey, "All Dressed Up with No Urge to Learn," *Atlanta Journal-Constitution*, December 8, 2008.

———, "Student Journalists . . . Need to Learn First Amendment Is Shield for Free Speech, Not Cocoon for Ignorance, Vulgarity," *Atlanta Journal-Constitution*, October 3, 2007.

*The Economist*, "Badge of Honour? School Uniforms," September 26, 2009.

Scott Forsyth, "Commentary: Students' Speech Not Free Online," *Daily Record* (Rochester, NY), February 9, 2010.

Charles C. Haynes, "For High School Students, Free Speech Is No Joke," First Amendment Center, July 8, 2007. www .firstamendmentcenter.org.

Frederick M. Hess, "Do Student Rights Interfere with Teaching and Learning in Public Schools?" *CQ Researcher*, June 1, 2009.

Julie Hilden, "How Should Teens' 'Sexting'—the Sending of Revealing Photos—Be Regulated?" *FindLaw*, April 28, 2009. www.findlaw.com.

Tom Jacobs, "10 Supreme Court Cases Every Teen Should Know: Part 1," *New York Times Upfront*, September 3, 2010.

———, "10 Supreme Court Cases Every Teen Should Know: Part 2," *New York Times Upfront*, September 17, 2010.

Suzanne Kapner, "Dress Code," *Fortune*, August 31, 2009.

Bonnie A. Kellman, "Tinkering with *Tinker*: Protecting the First Amendment in Public Schools," *Notre Dame Law Review*, 2009.

Janet Kornblum and Beth Marklein, "What You Say Online Could Haunt You," *USA Today*, March 8, 2006.

Frank D. LoMonte, "Student Journalism Confronts a New Generation of Legal Challenges," *Human Rights*, Summer 2008.

David L. Martinson, "Vulgar, Indecent, and Offensive Student Speech: How Should Public School Administrators Respond?" *The Clearing House*, 1998.

E.Y. Meyer and Jack Hayes, "The Case for Hate," *Life*, Fall 1991.

Andrea Otanez, "Giving Student Journalists Ownership of Their Papers," *Seattle Times*, January 31, 2007.

Robert S. Peck and Ann K. Symons, "Kids Have First Amendment Rights, Too," *American Libraries*, September 1997.

*Spokesman-Review* (Spokane, WA), "Free Speech 4 Teens: Even Silly Antics Deserve First Amendment Rights," July 1, 2007.

*USA Today*, "Our View on Freedom of Expression: Protect Student Speech—Even 'Unwise' Bong Banner," March 21, 2007.

Kathryn S. Vander Broek, Steven M. Puiszis, and Evan D. Brown, "Schools and Social Media: First Amendment Issues Arising from Student Use of the Internet," *Intellectual Property & Technology Law Journal*, April 2009.

Alistair Waters, "Privilege of Free Speech Should Be Balanced with Respect," *Kelowna Capital News* (Kelowna, British Columbia), September 28, 2010.

Thomas E. Wheeler II, "Slamming in Cyberspace: The Boundaries of Student First Amendment Rights," *Computer & Internet Lawyer*, April 2004.

Joann Wypijewski, "Through a Lens Starkly," *Nation*, May 18, 2009.

# Index